50 Bread Baking Beyond Basic Recipes for Home

By: Kelly Johnson

Table of Contents

- Classic French Baguette
- Sourdough Boule
- Whole Wheat Sandwich Loaf
- Rye Bread with Caraway Seeds
- Challah Bread
- Ciabatta Loaf
- Multigrain Bread
- Focaccia with Herbs and Olive Oil
- Cinnamon Raisin Bread
- Potato Bread
- Brioche Loaf
- Pumpernickel Bread
- Pretzels
- English Muffins
- Naan Bread
- Garlic Knots
- Irish Soda Bread
- Whole Grain Dinner Rolls
- Bagels
- Cranberry Walnut Bread
- Pizza Dough
- Cornbread
- Swedish Limpa Bread
- Portuguese Sweet Bread
- Parker House Rolls
- Cheese Bread
- Olive Bread
- Sunflower Seed Bread
- Pita Bread
- Whole Wheat Challah
- Honey Oat Bread
- Pretzel Rolls
- Rosemary Olive Oil Bread
- Raisin Bread
- Anadama Bread
- Cinnamon Swirl Bread

- Hokkaido Milk Bread
- Beer Bread
- Jalapeño Cheddar Bread
- Onion Rye Bread
- Whole Wheat Baguettes
- Sourdough English Muffins
- Gluten-Free Bread
- Spelt Bread
- Lavash Crackers
- Swedish Cardamom Bread
- Lemon Poppy Seed Bread
- Pistachio Cranberry Bread
- Chocolate Babka
- Stollen

Classic French Baguette

Ingredients:

- 500g bread flour (approximately 4 cups)
- 10g salt (about 2 teaspoons)
- 10g instant yeast (about 2 teaspoons)
- 350ml water (approximately 1.5 cups)

Instructions:

1. **Mixing the Dough:**
   - In a large bowl, combine the bread flour, salt, and instant yeast.
   - Gradually add the water while mixing with a spoon or dough whisk until a rough dough forms.
2. **Kneading:**
   - Transfer the dough to a lightly floured surface and knead for about 10-15 minutes until the dough becomes smooth and elastic. You can also use a stand mixer fitted with a dough hook for this step.
3. **First Rise (Bulk Fermentation):**
   - Place the dough in a lightly oiled bowl and cover with plastic wrap or a damp kitchen towel.
   - Let it rise at room temperature for about 1.5 to 2 hours, or until doubled in size.
4. **Shaping:**
   - Once risen, gently deflate the dough and divide it into 3 equal portions for classic baguettes.
   - Shape each portion into a rough rectangle, then fold the sides towards the center and roll it up tightly from the top to the bottom, sealing the seam well.
5. **Final Rise:**
   - Place the shaped baguettes on a floured surface or a couche (a floured cloth) and cover with plastic wrap or a towel.
   - Let them rise for another 45 minutes to 1 hour, or until puffy.
6. **Preheat the Oven:**
   - About 30 minutes before baking, preheat your oven to 450°F (230°C). Place a baking stone or an upside-down baking sheet in the oven to preheat as well.
7. **Scoring and Baking:**
   - Using a sharp knife or a bread lame, make 3-4 diagonal slashes along the top of each baguette.
   - Quickly transfer the baguettes onto the preheated baking stone or sheet.
   - Optionally, you can create steam in the oven by spraying water onto the sides of the oven or placing a tray with ice cubes on the bottom rack.
8. **Baking:**
   - Bake the baguettes for 20-25 minutes, or until they are golden brown and sound hollow when tapped on the bottom.

9. **Cooling:**
   - Transfer the baguettes to a wire rack to cool completely before slicing. This helps retain their crisp crust.

Tips:

- **Flour Type:** Bread flour is preferred for baguettes as it has higher protein content, which helps in gluten development and structure.
- **Steam:** Creating steam in the oven during baking helps in forming a crispy crust. Be cautious when handling steam.
- **Scoring:** Proper scoring allows the dough to expand evenly during baking and gives the baguettes their characteristic appearance.
- **Storage:** Baguettes are best enjoyed fresh on the day they are baked. If storing, wrap them loosely in a paper bag to maintain the crust's crispness.

Enjoy your homemade classic French baguettes!

Sourdough Boule

Ingredients:

For the Sourdough Starter:

- 50g active sourdough starter (100% hydration)
- 100g bread flour
- 100g water

For the Dough:

- 350g bread flour
- 200g water
- 9g salt

Instructions:

Day 1: Prepare the Sourdough Starter

1. **Feed Your Starter:** Take 50g of your active sourdough starter (maintained at 100% hydration, meaning equal parts flour and water by weight) and combine it with 100g of bread flour and 100g of water in a bowl. Mix well until fully combined to form a stiff dough.
2. **Ferment the Starter:** Cover the bowl loosely and let it sit at room temperature (ideally around 70-75°F or 21-24°C) for about 4-6 hours, or until it doubles in size and becomes bubbly and active.
3. **Refrigerate the Starter:** Once the starter is active, you can either proceed with making the dough or refrigerate the starter overnight to develop more flavor. If refrigerating, take it out 1-2 hours before mixing the dough to bring it back to room temperature.

Day 2: Making the Dough

1. **Mixing the Dough:**
    - In a large mixing bowl, combine 350g of bread flour and 200g of water. Mix until all the flour is hydrated and a shaggy dough forms. Cover with a kitchen towel or plastic wrap and let it rest for 30-60 minutes (autolyse).
2. **Incorporate the Starter:**
    - Add the 50g of active sourdough starter (the remainder after feeding) to the dough mixture. Mix until the starter is evenly distributed throughout the dough.
3. **Add Salt:**
    - Sprinkle 9g of salt over the dough. You can dissolve the salt in a little water before adding it to ensure even distribution.
4. **Bulk Fermentation:**

- Perform a series of stretch and folds every 30 minutes for the first 2 hours. To stretch and fold, wet your hands, grab one side of the dough, stretch it upwards, and fold it over to the opposite side. Repeat this process from all four sides of the dough.
5. **Final Proof:**
    - After the bulk fermentation, shape the dough into a boule (round loaf). To shape, lightly flour your work surface, gently pat the dough into a rectangle, fold the edges towards the center, then shape into a tight ball.
6. **Second Rise (Proofing):**
    - Place the shaped boule in a proofing basket or a bowl lined with a well-floured kitchen towel, seam side up. Cover loosely with plastic wrap or a kitchen towel and let it rise at room temperature for about 3-4 hours, or until it increases in size by about 50-75%.
7. **Preheat the Oven:**
    - About 30 minutes before baking, preheat your oven to 450°F (230°C). Place a baking stone or a Dutch oven (if using) in the oven to preheat as well.
8. **Score and Bake:**
    - Once the dough has finished proofing, carefully transfer it onto a piece of parchment paper. Score the top of the boule with a sharp knife or a bread lame in a pattern of your choice.
9. **Baking:**
    - If using a baking stone, slide the parchment paper with the boule onto the preheated stone in the oven. If using a Dutch oven, carefully place the boule (with parchment paper) into the preheated Dutch oven, cover with the lid, and bake for 20 minutes. Then remove the lid and bake for an additional 20-25 minutes, or until the boule is golden brown and sounds hollow when tapped on the bottom.
10. **Cooling:**
    - Transfer the baked sourdough boule to a wire rack and let it cool completely before slicing. This helps in retaining the moisture and texture of the bread.

Tips:

- **Starter Maintenance:** Ensure your sourdough starter is active and healthy before using it in the recipe.
- **Autolyse:** Allowing the flour and water to rest before adding the starter and salt improves gluten development and texture.
- **Proofing:** The dough should roughly double in size during the final proof. If you gently press your finger into the dough and it springs back slowly, it's ready to bake.
- **Baking Equipment:** A baking stone or Dutch oven helps create a steamy environment for a crispy crust.
- **Storage:** Once cooled, store the sourdough boule in a paper bag or bread box to maintain its crust.

Enjoy your homemade sourdough boule with its tangy flavor and rustic crust!

Whole Wheat Sandwich Loaf

Ingredients:

- 400g whole wheat flour
- 100g bread flour (or all-purpose flour)
- 10g salt (about 2 teaspoons)
- 10g instant yeast (about 2 teaspoons)
- 30g honey or sugar (about 2 tablespoons)
- 350ml warm water (about 1.5 cups)
- 30g unsalted butter, softened (about 2 tablespoons)

Instructions:

1. **Activate the Yeast:**
   - In a small bowl, mix the warm water (around 110°F or 43°C), honey (or sugar), and instant yeast. Let it sit for about 5-10 minutes until frothy and bubbly.
2. **Mixing the Dough:**
   - In a large mixing bowl or the bowl of a stand mixer fitted with a dough hook, combine the whole wheat flour, bread flour (or all-purpose flour), and salt.
3. **Combine the Ingredients:**
   - Add the activated yeast mixture and softened butter to the flour mixture. Mix until a rough dough forms.
4. **Kneading:**
   - Knead the dough for about 10-12 minutes by hand on a lightly floured surface, or 8-10 minutes using a stand mixer on medium-low speed. The dough should become smooth, elastic, and slightly tacky.
5. **First Rise (Bulk Fermentation):**
   - Place the kneaded dough in a lightly oiled bowl, cover with a kitchen towel or plastic wrap, and let it rise in a warm, draft-free place for about 1 to 1.5 hours, or until doubled in size.
6. **Shaping:**
   - Grease a 9x5 inch loaf pan. Gently deflate the risen dough and shape it into a loaf that fits the pan. Place it seam side down into the prepared loaf pan.
7. **Second Rise:**
   - Cover the loaf pan loosely with plastic wrap or a kitchen towel and let the dough rise again for about 45 minutes to 1 hour, or until it rises just above the rim of the pan.
8. **Preheat the Oven:**
   - About 30 minutes before baking, preheat your oven to 375°F (190°C).
9. **Baking:**
   - Bake the loaf in the preheated oven for 30-35 minutes, or until the top is golden brown and the loaf sounds hollow when tapped on the bottom.
10. **Cooling:**

- Remove the bread from the pan and transfer it to a wire rack to cool completely before slicing. This helps to maintain its structure and texture.

Tips:

- **Flour Types:** Using a combination of whole wheat flour and bread flour (or all-purpose flour) helps to balance the texture and rise of the bread.
- **Sweetener:** Honey adds flavor and helps with the yeast activation. You can substitute with sugar if preferred.
- **Butter:** Butter enriches the dough, giving the bread a softer texture and adding flavor.
- **Rising Time:** Times may vary depending on your kitchen temperature. Ensure the dough has doubled in size during both rises for the best results.
- **Storage:** Once cooled, store the whole wheat sandwich loaf in a plastic bag or bread box at room temperature for up to 3-4 days. You can also slice and freeze it for longer storage.

Enjoy your homemade whole wheat sandwich loaf for delicious sandwiches or toasted slices with your favorite spreads!

Rye Bread with Caraway Seeds

Ingredients:

- 300g rye flour
- 200g bread flour (or all-purpose flour)
- 10g salt (about 2 teaspoons)
- 10g instant yeast (about 2 teaspoons)
- 10g caraway seeds (about 1 tablespoon)
- 30g molasses or honey (about 2 tablespoons)
- 30g unsalted butter, softened (about 2 tablespoons)
- 350ml warm water (about 1.5 cups)

Instructions:

1. **Activate the Yeast:**
   - In a small bowl, mix the warm water (around 110°F or 43°C), molasses (or honey), and instant yeast. Let it sit for about 5-10 minutes until frothy and bubbly.
2. **Mixing the Dough:**
   - In a large mixing bowl or the bowl of a stand mixer fitted with a dough hook, combine the rye flour, bread flour (or all-purpose flour), salt, and caraway seeds.
3. **Combine Ingredients:**
   - Add the activated yeast mixture and softened butter to the flour mixture. Mix until a rough dough forms.
4. **Kneading:**
   - Knead the dough for about 10-12 minutes by hand on a lightly floured surface, or 8-10 minutes using a stand mixer on medium-low speed. The dough should become smooth, elastic, and slightly tacky.
5. **First Rise (Bulk Fermentation):**
   - Place the kneaded dough in a lightly oiled bowl, cover with a kitchen towel or plastic wrap, and let it rise in a warm, draft-free place for about 1 to 1.5 hours, or until doubled in size.
6. **Shaping:**
   - Grease a baking sheet or line it with parchment paper. Gently deflate the risen dough and shape it into a round or oval loaf. Place it on the prepared baking sheet.
7. **Second Rise:**
   - Cover the loaf loosely with plastic wrap or a kitchen towel and let it rise again for about 45 minutes to 1 hour, or until it rises and spreads slightly.
8. **Preheat the Oven:**
   - About 30 minutes before baking, preheat your oven to 375°F (190°C).
9. **Baking:**
   - Optional: Before baking, you can brush the top of the loaf with water and sprinkle some additional caraway seeds for extra flavor and decoration.

- Bake the loaf in the preheated oven for 30-35 minutes, or until the top is golden brown and the loaf sounds hollow when tapped on the bottom.
10. **Cooling:**
    - Transfer the rye bread to a wire rack to cool completely before slicing. This helps to maintain its structure and texture.

Tips:

- **Flour Types:** Using a combination of rye flour and bread flour (or all-purpose flour) helps to balance the texture and rise of the bread.
- **Caraway Seeds:** Adjust the amount of caraway seeds to your preference. They add a distinctive flavor that complements rye bread wonderfully.
- **Sweetener:** Molasses adds depth of flavor, but you can substitute with honey or even brown sugar if preferred.
- **Butter:** Butter enriches the dough, giving the bread a softer texture and adding flavor.
- **Rising Time:** Times may vary depending on your kitchen temperature. Ensure the dough has doubled in size during both rises for the best results.
- **Storage:** Once cooled, store the rye bread in a plastic bag or bread box at room temperature for up to 3-4 days. You can also slice and freeze it for longer storage.

Enjoy your homemade rye bread with caraway seeds! It's perfect for sandwiches, toast, or simply enjoyed with butter.

Challah Bread

Ingredients:

- 500g bread flour
- 10g salt (about 2 teaspoons)
- 15g instant yeast (about 1 tablespoon)
- 3 large eggs, plus 1 egg for egg wash
- 75g granulated sugar (about 1/3 cup)
- 120ml vegetable oil (about 1/2 cup)
- 180ml lukewarm water (about 3/4 cup)
- Sesame seeds or poppy seeds (optional, for topping)

Instructions:

1. **Activate the Yeast:**
   - In a small bowl, mix the lukewarm water, sugar, and instant yeast. Let it sit for about 5-10 minutes until frothy and bubbly.
2. **Mixing the Dough:**
   - In a large mixing bowl or the bowl of a stand mixer fitted with a dough hook, combine the bread flour and salt.
   - Make a well in the center and add the eggs (reserve one for egg wash), vegetable oil, and the activated yeast mixture.
3. **Kneading:**
   - Mix the ingredients until a rough dough forms. Knead the dough for about 10-12 minutes by hand on a lightly floured surface, or 8-10 minutes using a stand mixer on medium-low speed. The dough should become smooth, elastic, and slightly tacky.
4. **First Rise (Bulk Fermentation):**
   - Place the kneaded dough in a lightly oiled bowl, cover with a kitchen towel or plastic wrap, and let it rise in a warm, draft-free place for about 1 to 1.5 hours, or until doubled in size.
5. **Shaping:**
   - After the first rise, gently deflate the dough and divide it into three equal portions for braiding.
   - Roll each portion into a long rope, about 16-18 inches long.
6. **Braiding:**
   - Line a baking sheet with parchment paper. Place the three ropes side by side and pinch them together at one end.
   - Braid the ropes together, just like braiding hair, and pinch the ends together when finished.
7. **Final Rise:**

- Place the braided loaf on the prepared baking sheet. Cover loosely with plastic wrap or a kitchen towel and let it rise again for about 45 minutes to 1 hour, or until it doubles in size.

8. **Preheat the Oven:**
    - About 30 minutes before baking, preheat your oven to 375°F (190°C).
9. **Egg Wash and Topping:**
    - In a small bowl, beat the remaining egg with a tablespoon of water to create an egg wash.
    - Brush the surface of the risen challah loaf with the egg wash. Optionally, sprinkle sesame seeds or poppy seeds on top for decoration.
10. **Baking:**
    - Bake the challah in the preheated oven for 25-30 minutes, or until the top is golden brown and the loaf sounds hollow when tapped on the bottom.
11. **Cooling:**
    - Transfer the baked challah bread to a wire rack to cool completely before slicing. This helps to maintain its texture and flavor.

Tips:

- **Eggs:** Using eggs in the dough enriches the bread, giving it a soft and tender crumb.
- **Sweetness:** The amount of sugar can be adjusted to your preference, depending on how sweet you like your challah.
- **Braiding:** There are various ways to braid challah, from a simple three-strand braid to more intricate designs. Choose a style that you prefer.
- **Variations:** Challah can also be flavored with additions like raisins, cinnamon, or even savory herbs for different variations.

Enjoy your homemade challah bread fresh or toasted, with butter or as part of your favorite sandwiches. It's a versatile and delightful bread that's perfect for any occasion!

Ciabatta Loaf

Ingredients:

- 500g bread flour
- 10g salt (about 2 teaspoons)
- 10g instant yeast (about 2 teaspoons)
- 400ml lukewarm water (about 1 and 2/3 cups)
- Extra virgin olive oil, for greasing and drizzling

Instructions:

1. **Mixing the Dough:**
   - In a large mixing bowl or the bowl of a stand mixer fitted with a dough hook, combine the bread flour, salt, and instant yeast.
   - Gradually add the lukewarm water while mixing on low speed (if using a stand mixer) or with a spoon or dough whisk, until all the flour is hydrated and a wet, sticky dough forms.
2. **Kneading:**
   - Continue kneading the dough for about 10-12 minutes by hand on a well-floured surface or 8-10 minutes using a stand mixer on medium-low speed. The dough will be very sticky but should start to come together and feel elastic.
3. **First Rise (Bulk Fermentation):**
   - Transfer the dough to a large, lightly oiled bowl. Cover with plastic wrap or a kitchen towel and let it rise in a warm, draft-free place for about 1.5 to 2 hours, or until doubled in size. The dough will be very bubbly and airy.
4. **Shaping:**
   - Line a baking sheet with parchment paper and lightly dust it with flour.
   - Using a dough scraper or spatula, gently deflate the dough and transfer it to the prepared baking sheet. Try to handle the dough gently to preserve the air bubbles.
5. **Second Rise:**
   - Let the shaped dough rise again for about 30-45 minutes, or until it becomes puffy. It won't double in size like some other breads, but it should visibly puff up.
6. **Preheat the Oven:**
   - About 30 minutes before baking, preheat your oven to 450°F (230°C). Place a baking stone or an upside-down baking sheet on the middle rack of the oven to preheat as well.
7. **Baking:**
   - Just before baking, drizzle some extra virgin olive oil over the top of the dough for added flavor and a crispy crust.
   - Bake the ciabatta in the preheated oven for 20-25 minutes, or until it is golden brown and sounds hollow when tapped on the bottom. Optionally, you can create

steam in the oven by spraying water onto the sides of the oven or placing a tray with ice cubes on the bottom rack.

8. **Cooling:**
   - Transfer the baked ciabatta loaf to a wire rack to cool completely before slicing. This helps to preserve its texture and crust.

Tips:

- **Wet Dough:** Ciabatta dough is intentionally wet to achieve its characteristic airy crumb and open holes. Resist the urge to add more flour during kneading.
- **Handling:** Use a dough scraper or spatula to handle the dough gently to preserve the air bubbles created during fermentation.
- **Baking Surface:** A baking stone or preheated baking sheet helps to create a crisp bottom crust. If you don't have one, you can bake the ciabatta directly on a parchment-lined baking sheet.
- **Storage:** Store the cooled ciabatta bread in a paper bag or bread box at room temperature for up to 2-3 days. It's best enjoyed fresh but can be refreshed by heating it in the oven for a few minutes before serving.

Ciabatta bread is wonderful for sandwiches, dipping into olive oil and balsamic vinegar, or simply enjoyed with butter. Its rustic appearance and delicious flavor make it a favorite among bread enthusiasts.

Multigrain Bread

Ingredients:

- 300g bread flour
- 150g whole wheat flour
- 50g rolled oats
- 30g flaxseeds
- 30g sunflower seeds
- 30g sesame seeds
- 10g salt (about 2 teaspoons)
- 10g instant yeast (about 2 teaspoons)
- 30g honey or molasses (about 2 tablespoons)
- 40g unsalted butter, softened (about 3 tablespoons)
- 350ml lukewarm water (about 1.5 cups)

Instructions:

1. **Activate the Yeast:**
    - In a small bowl, mix the lukewarm water, honey (or molasses), and instant yeast. Let it sit for about 5-10 minutes until frothy and bubbly.
2. **Prepare the Grains and Seeds:**
    - In a separate bowl, combine the rolled oats, flaxseeds, sunflower seeds, and sesame seeds. Mix well and set aside.
3. **Mixing the Dough:**
    - In a large mixing bowl or the bowl of a stand mixer fitted with a dough hook, combine the bread flour, whole wheat flour, salt, and softened butter.
    - Add the activated yeast mixture and mix until a rough dough forms.
4. **Incorporate Grains and Seeds:**
    - Gradually add the mixed grains and seeds to the dough mixture. Knead the dough until all ingredients are well combined and the dough becomes smooth and elastic. This may take about 10-12 minutes by hand or 8-10 minutes using a stand mixer on medium-low speed.
5. **First Rise (Bulk Fermentation):**
    - Place the kneaded dough in a lightly oiled bowl, cover with plastic wrap or a kitchen towel, and let it rise in a warm, draft-free place for about 1.5 to 2 hours, or until doubled in size.
6. **Shaping:**
    - Gently deflate the risen dough and shape it into a loaf. You can use a loaf pan or shape it freeform on a parchment-lined baking sheet.
7. **Second Rise:**
    - Cover the shaped loaf loosely with plastic wrap or a kitchen towel and let it rise again for about 45 minutes to 1 hour, or until it increases in size by about 50-75%.

8. **Preheat the Oven:**
   - About 30 minutes before baking, preheat your oven to 375°F (190°C).
9. **Baking:**
   - Bake the multigrain bread in the preheated oven for 30-35 minutes, or until the top is golden brown and the loaf sounds hollow when tapped on the bottom.
10. **Cooling:**
    - Transfer the baked multigrain bread to a wire rack to cool completely before slicing. This helps to maintain its structure and texture.

Tips:

- **Variety of Grains:** Feel free to adjust the types of grains and seeds used based on your preference. You can add or substitute with ingredients like chia seeds, pumpkin seeds, or millet.
- **Sweetener:** Honey or molasses adds a touch of sweetness and enhances the flavor of the bread. You can adjust the amount based on your taste.
- **Butter:** Softened butter enriches the dough and contributes to its soft texture.
- **Storage:** Once cooled, store the multigrain bread in a paper bag or bread box at room temperature for up to 3-4 days. It can also be sliced and frozen for longer storage.

Enjoy your homemade multigrain bread toasted with butter, used for sandwiches, or paired with soups and salads. Its wholesome flavor and hearty texture make it a nutritious choice for any meal!

Focaccia with Herbs and Olive Oil

Ingredients:

- 500g bread flour
- 10g salt (about 2 teaspoons)
- 10g instant yeast (about 2 teaspoons)
- 375ml lukewarm water (about 1.5 cups)
- 60ml extra virgin olive oil (about 1/4 cup), plus extra for drizzling
- 2-3 tablespoons fresh herbs (such as rosemary, thyme, oregano, or a mix), chopped
- Coarse sea salt, for sprinkling on top

Instructions:

1. **Activate the Yeast:**
   - In a small bowl, mix the lukewarm water and instant yeast. Let it sit for about 5-10 minutes until frothy and bubbly.
2. **Mixing the Dough:**
   - In a large mixing bowl or the bowl of a stand mixer fitted with a dough hook, combine the bread flour and salt.
   - Add the activated yeast mixture and olive oil to the flour mixture. Mix until a rough dough forms.
3. **Kneading:**
   - Knead the dough for about 10-12 minutes by hand on a well-floured surface, or 8-10 minutes using a stand mixer on medium-low speed. The dough should become smooth, elastic, and slightly tacky.
4. **First Rise (Bulk Fermentation):**
   - Place the kneaded dough in a lightly oiled bowl, cover with plastic wrap or a kitchen towel, and let it rise in a warm, draft-free place for about 1 to 1.5 hours, or until doubled in size.
5. **Shaping:**
   - Lightly grease a baking sheet (approximately 9x13 inches) with olive oil.
   - Gently deflate the risen dough and transfer it to the prepared baking sheet. Using your fingertips, press the dough out evenly to fill the pan. If the dough springs back, let it rest for 10-15 minutes and then continue pressing.
6. **Second Rise:**
   - Cover the shaped dough loosely with plastic wrap or a kitchen towel and let it rise again for about 30-45 minutes, or until it becomes puffy and increases slightly in thickness.
7. **Preheat the Oven:**
   - About 30 minutes before baking, preheat your oven to 425°F (220°C).
8. **Adding Herbs and Olive Oil:**

- Once the dough has completed its second rise, gently dimple the surface of the dough with your fingertips. Drizzle the top generously with extra virgin olive oil, allowing it to pool in the indentations.
- Sprinkle the chopped fresh herbs evenly over the top of the dough.
- Finally, sprinkle coarse sea salt evenly over the dough.

9. **Baking:**
   - Bake the focaccia in the preheated oven for 20-25 minutes, or until the top is golden brown and the bread sounds hollow when tapped on the bottom.

10. **Cooling:**
    - Transfer the baked focaccia to a wire rack to cool slightly before slicing and serving. It's best enjoyed warm.

Tips:

- **Herbs:** Use a combination of your favorite fresh herbs for maximum flavor. Rosemary is a classic choice, but thyme, oregano, or a mix of herbs can also be wonderful.
- **Olive Oil:** Extra virgin olive oil not only adds flavor but also contributes to the soft texture and golden crust of the focaccia.
- **Sea Salt:** Coarse sea salt sprinkled on top enhances the savory flavor and adds a nice crunch.
- **Storage:** Focaccia is best enjoyed fresh on the day it is baked. If you have leftovers, store them in an airtight container at room temperature for up to 2 days, or freeze slices wrapped well in plastic wrap and foil.

Enjoy your homemade focaccia with herbs and olive oil as a delightful addition to any meal or as a tasty snack!

Cinnamon Raisin Bread

Ingredients:

- 500g bread flour
- 10g salt (about 2 teaspoons)
- 10g instant yeast (about 2 teaspoons)
- 50g granulated sugar (about 1/4 cup)
- 300ml lukewarm milk (about 1 and 1/4 cups)
- 50g unsalted butter, softened (about 3.5 tablespoons)
- 1 large egg
- 1 teaspoon vanilla extract
- 150g raisins (about 1 cup)
- 2 tablespoons ground cinnamon
- 50g brown sugar (about 1/4 cup)

Instructions:

1. **Activate the Yeast:**
    - In a small bowl, mix the lukewarm milk and granulated sugar. Sprinkle the instant yeast over the milk mixture and let it sit for about 5-10 minutes until frothy and bubbly.
2. **Mixing the Dough:**
    - In a large mixing bowl or the bowl of a stand mixer fitted with a dough hook, combine the bread flour and salt.
    - Add the activated yeast mixture, softened butter, egg, and vanilla extract to the flour mixture. Mix until a rough dough forms.
3. **Kneading:**
    - Knead the dough for about 10-12 minutes by hand on a well-floured surface, or 8-10 minutes using a stand mixer on medium-low speed. The dough should become smooth, elastic, and slightly tacky.
4. **Incorporating Raisins and Cinnamon:**
    - During the last few minutes of kneading, gradually add the raisins, ground cinnamon, and brown sugar to the dough. Knead until the raisins and cinnamon sugar are evenly distributed throughout the dough.
5. **First Rise (Bulk Fermentation):**
    - Place the kneaded dough in a lightly oiled bowl, cover with plastic wrap or a kitchen towel, and let it rise in a warm, draft-free place for about 1 to 1.5 hours, or until doubled in size.
6. **Shaping:**
    - Gently deflate the risen dough and turn it out onto a lightly floured surface. Divide the dough in half and shape each half into a loaf.

- Place each loaf into a greased 9x5 inch loaf pan. Cover loosely with plastic wrap or a kitchen towel and let them rise again for about 30-45 minutes, or until they rise just above the rim of the pans.
7. **Preheat the Oven:**
    - About 30 minutes before baking, preheat your oven to 375°F (190°C).
8. **Baking:**
    - Bake the loaves in the preheated oven for 30-35 minutes, or until the tops are golden brown and the loaves sound hollow when tapped on the bottom.
9. **Cooling:**
    - Remove the cinnamon raisin bread from the pans and transfer them to a wire rack to cool completely before slicing. This helps to maintain their structure and texture.

Tips:

- **Raisins:** You can plump the raisins before adding them to the dough by soaking them in hot water or rum for about 10-15 minutes, then draining them well.
- **Cinnamon Sugar Swirl:** For a more pronounced cinnamon flavor, mix some extra cinnamon with sugar and sprinkle it over the rolled-out dough before rolling it up.
- **Storage:** Store the cooled cinnamon raisin bread in a plastic bag or bread box at room temperature for up to 3-4 days. It can also be sliced and frozen for longer storage.

Enjoy your homemade cinnamon raisin bread toasted with butter for breakfast, or use it to make delicious sandwiches. Its sweet and aromatic flavor makes it a favorite for all occasions!

Potato Bread

Ingredients:

- 300g mashed potatoes (about 2 medium potatoes, peeled, boiled, and mashed)
- 500g bread flour
- 10g salt (about 2 teaspoons)
- 10g instant yeast (about 2 teaspoons)
- 50g granulated sugar (about 1/4 cup)
- 60ml unsalted butter, melted (about 1/4 cup)
- 240ml lukewarm milk (about 1 cup)
- 1 large egg

Instructions:

1. **Prepare the Mashed Potatoes:**
    - Peel, chop, and boil the potatoes until tender. Drain and mash them until smooth. Measure out 300g of mashed potatoes for the recipe.
2. **Activate the Yeast:**
    - In a small bowl, mix the lukewarm milk and granulated sugar. Sprinkle the instant yeast over the milk mixture and let it sit for about 5-10 minutes until frothy and bubbly.
3. **Mixing the Dough:**
    - In a large mixing bowl or the bowl of a stand mixer fitted with a dough hook, combine the bread flour and salt.
    - Add the melted butter, mashed potatoes, activated yeast mixture, and egg to the flour mixture. Mix until a rough dough forms.
4. **Kneading:**
    - Knead the dough for about 10-12 minutes by hand on a well-floured surface, or 8-10 minutes using a stand mixer on medium-low speed. The dough should become smooth, elastic, and slightly tacky.
5. **First Rise (Bulk Fermentation):**
    - Place the kneaded dough in a lightly oiled bowl, cover with plastic wrap or a kitchen towel, and let it rise in a warm, draft-free place for about 1 to 1.5 hours, or until doubled in size.
6. **Shaping:**
    - Gently deflate the risen dough and turn it out onto a lightly floured surface. Divide the dough in half and shape each half into a loaf.
    - Place each loaf into a greased 9x5 inch loaf pan. Cover loosely with plastic wrap or a kitchen towel and let them rise again for about 30-45 minutes, or until they rise just above the rim of the pans.
7. **Preheat the Oven:**
    - About 30 minutes before baking, preheat your oven to 375°F (190°C).
8. **Baking:**

- Bake the loaves in the preheated oven for 30-35 minutes, or until the tops are golden brown and the loaves sound hollow when tapped on the bottom.

9. **Cooling:**
   - Remove the potato bread from the pans and transfer them to a wire rack to cool completely before slicing. This helps to maintain their structure and texture.

Tips:

- **Potatoes:** Use starchy potatoes like Russet or Yukon Gold for the best texture in the bread.
- **Butter:** Melted butter adds richness and flavor to the dough.
- **Variations:** You can add herbs, cheese, or even mix in some whole grains like oats or seeds for added texture and flavor.
- **Storage:** Store the cooled potato bread in a plastic bag or bread box at room temperature for up to 3-4 days. It can also be sliced and frozen for longer storage.

Enjoy your homemade potato bread fresh or toasted with butter or your favorite spreads. Its soft texture and subtle sweetness make it a versatile choice for sandwiches or enjoying on its own!

Brioche Loaf

Ingredients:

- 500g bread flour
- 10g salt (about 2 teaspoons)
- 50g granulated sugar (about 1/4 cup)
- 10g instant yeast (about 2 teaspoons)
- 5 large eggs, at room temperature
- 200g unsalted butter, softened but still cool (about 14 tablespoons)
- 60ml lukewarm milk (about 1/4 cup)
- 1 egg, beaten (for egg wash)

Instructions:

1. **Mixing the Dough:**
   - In a large mixing bowl or the bowl of a stand mixer fitted with a dough hook, combine the bread flour, salt, sugar, and instant yeast.
   - Add the eggs one at a time, mixing well after each addition.
   - Continue mixing until the dough comes together.
2. **Incorporating Butter:**
   - Gradually add the softened butter, a few tablespoons at a time, while continuing to mix the dough on medium speed. It may seem like the butter is not incorporating at first, but keep mixing and it will come together into a smooth and elastic dough.
3. **Kneading:**
   - Knead the dough for about 15-20 minutes in the stand mixer on medium speed, or turn the dough out onto a lightly floured surface and knead by hand until the dough is very smooth, elastic, and no longer sticky.
4. **First Rise (Bulk Fermentation):**
   - Place the kneaded dough in a large, lightly oiled bowl. Cover with plastic wrap or a kitchen towel and let it rise in a warm, draft-free place for about 1.5 to 2 hours, or until doubled in size.
5. **Shaping:**
   - Gently deflate the risen dough and turn it out onto a lightly floured surface. Shape it into a loaf and place it into a greased 9x5 inch loaf pan.
   - Alternatively, you can shape the dough into small brioche rolls or use it to make brioche buns.
6. **Second Rise:**
   - Cover the shaped dough loosely with plastic wrap or a kitchen towel and let it rise again for about 1 to 1.5 hours, or until it doubles in size and fills the loaf pan.
7. **Preheat the Oven:**
   - About 30 minutes before baking, preheat your oven to 375°F (190°C).
8. **Baking:**

- Brush the top of the brioche loaf with beaten egg to create a shiny crust.
- Bake in the preheated oven for 30-35 minutes, or until the top is golden brown and the loaf sounds hollow when tapped on the bottom.

9. **Cooling:**
   - Remove the brioche loaf from the pan and transfer it to a wire rack to cool completely before slicing. This helps to maintain its structure and texture.

Tips:

- **Room Temperature Ingredients:** Ensure that the eggs and butter are at room temperature before starting to mix the dough. This helps in achieving a smooth and uniform dough.
- **Butter Incorporation:** Take your time when incorporating the butter into the dough. It's normal for the dough to look messy or greasy at first, but continue mixing until it becomes smooth and elastic.
- **Variations:** Brioche is versatile and can be shaped into various forms like rolls, buns, or even braided loaves. You can also add flavors like vanilla extract or orange zest for a different twist.
- **Storage:** Store the cooled brioche loaf in a plastic bag or bread box at room temperature for up to 3-4 days. It can also be sliced and frozen for longer storage.

Enjoy your homemade brioche loaf as a delightful treat for breakfast or as a base for sandwiches. Its rich and buttery flavor makes it a favorite for any occasion!

Pumpernickel Bread

Ingredients:

- 250g rye flour
- 250g bread flour (or all-purpose flour)
- 10g salt (about 2 teaspoons)
- 10g instant yeast (about 2 teaspoons)
- 30g molasses
- 30g unsalted butter, softened (about 2 tablespoons)
- 300ml lukewarm water (about 1 and 1/4 cups)
- 30g cocoa powder (unsweetened)
- 1 tablespoon caraway seeds (optional, for flavor)

Instructions:

1. **Mixing the Dough:**
    - In a large mixing bowl or the bowl of a stand mixer fitted with a dough hook, combine the rye flour, bread flour, salt, instant yeast, molasses, softened butter, and lukewarm water.
    - Mix until a rough dough forms.
2. **Kneading:**
    - Knead the dough for about 10-12 minutes by hand on a well-floured surface, or 8-10 minutes using a stand mixer on medium-low speed. The dough should become smooth, elastic, and slightly tacky.
3. **Incorporate Cocoa Powder:**
    - Add the cocoa powder to the dough and continue kneading until it is fully incorporated. The cocoa powder will give the bread its characteristic dark color.
4. **First Rise (Bulk Fermentation):**
    - Place the kneaded dough in a lightly oiled bowl, cover with plastic wrap or a kitchen towel, and let it rise in a warm, draft-free place for about 1 to 1.5 hours, or until doubled in size.
5. **Shaping:**
    - Gently deflate the risen dough and shape it into a loaf. You can shape it into a traditional loaf shape or round shape, depending on your preference.
    - Place the shaped dough onto a parchment-lined baking sheet or into a greased loaf pan.
6. **Second Rise:**
    - Cover the shaped dough loosely with plastic wrap or a kitchen towel and let it rise again for about 30-45 minutes, or until it increases in size by about 50-75%.
7. **Preheat the Oven:**
    - About 30 minutes before baking, preheat your oven to 375°F (190°C).
8. **Baking:**

- Bake the pumpernickel bread in the preheated oven for 40-50 minutes, or until the top is firm and the loaf sounds hollow when tapped on the bottom.

9. **Cooling:**
   - Transfer the baked pumpernickel bread to a wire rack to cool completely before slicing. This helps to maintain its texture and flavor.

Tips:

- **Rye Flour:** Using a combination of rye flour and bread flour (or all-purpose flour) helps achieve the right texture and flavor balance.
- **Molasses:** Adds sweetness and contributes to the dark color of the bread. You can adjust the amount based on your preference for sweetness.
- **Cocoa Powder:** Gives the bread its characteristic dark color. Make sure to use unsweetened cocoa powder.
- **Caraway Seeds:** Optional but traditional in pumpernickel bread for added flavor. Feel free to adjust the amount to suit your taste.

Enjoy your homemade pumpernickel bread sliced thinly with cream cheese and smoked salmon, or use it as a base for hearty sandwiches. Its robust flavor and dense texture make it a satisfying choice for any meal!

Pretzels

Ingredients:

- 500g bread flour
- 10g salt (about 2 teaspoons)
- 10g granulated sugar (about 2 teaspoons)
- 10g instant yeast (about 2 teaspoons)
- 350ml lukewarm water (about 1.5 cups)
- 2 tablespoons baking soda
- Coarse sea salt, for sprinkling
- 1 egg, beaten (for egg wash)

Instructions:

1. **Mixing the Dough:**
   - In a large mixing bowl or the bowl of a stand mixer fitted with a dough hook, combine the bread flour, salt, sugar, and instant yeast.
   - Gradually add the lukewarm water while mixing, until a soft dough forms. You may not need all the water, so add it gradually and adjust as needed.
2. **Kneading:**
   - Knead the dough for about 8-10 minutes by hand on a well-floured surface, or 6-8 minutes using a stand mixer on medium-low speed. The dough should become smooth, elastic, and slightly tacky.
3. **First Rise (Bulk Fermentation):**
   - Place the kneaded dough in a lightly oiled bowl, cover with plastic wrap or a kitchen towel, and let it rise in a warm, draft-free place for about 1 hour, or until doubled in size.
4. **Shaping the Pretzels:**
   - Once the dough has risen, turn it out onto a lightly floured surface. Divide the dough into 8 equal portions.
   - Roll each portion into a long rope, about 20-22 inches (50-55 cm) long. Shape each rope into a pretzel: form a U-shape, then cross the ends over each other and press them down onto the bottom curve of the U to form the traditional pretzel shape.
5. **Second Rise:**
   - Place the shaped pretzels onto a parchment-lined baking sheet, leaving space between them. Cover loosely with plastic wrap or a kitchen towel and let them rise again for about 15-20 minutes.
6. **Boiling the Pretzels:**
   - Preheat your oven to 425°F (220°C). In a large pot, bring about 2 liters of water to a boil.
   - Once boiling, carefully add the baking soda to the water (it will bubble up briefly).

- Gently place each pretzel into the boiling water, one or two at a time, and boil for about 30 seconds on each side. Use a slotted spoon to remove them from the water and place them back onto the baking sheet.

7. **Baking:**
    - Brush each pretzel with beaten egg wash and sprinkle with coarse sea salt.
    - Bake in the preheated oven for 12-15 minutes, or until the pretzels are golden brown and have a slight sheen.
8. **Cooling:**
    - Transfer the baked pretzels to a wire rack to cool slightly before serving. Pretzels are best enjoyed warm.

Tips:

- **Shaping:** If you find it challenging to shape pretzels, you can also shape the dough into rolls or twists for a similar taste.
- **Toppings:** Experiment with different toppings such as sesame seeds, poppy seeds, or even cheese before baking.
- **Dipping Sauces:** Serve pretzels with mustard, cheese sauce, or any other dipping sauce of your choice for extra flavor.

Enjoy your homemade soft pretzels as a delicious snack or appetizer. Their chewy texture and salty crust make them a favorite treat for both kids and adults alike!

English Muffins

Ingredients:

- 350g bread flour
- 10g granulated sugar (about 2 teaspoons)
- 5g salt (about 1 teaspoon)
- 7g instant yeast (about 2 teaspoons)
- 30g unsalted butter, softened (about 2 tablespoons)
- 240ml lukewarm milk (about 1 cup)
- Cornmeal or semolina flour, for dusting

Instructions:

1. **Mixing the Dough:**
   - In a large mixing bowl or the bowl of a stand mixer fitted with a dough hook, combine the bread flour, sugar, salt, and instant yeast.
   - Add the softened butter and lukewarm milk. Mix until a rough dough forms.
2. **Kneading:**
   - Knead the dough for about 8-10 minutes by hand on a well-floured surface, or 6-8 minutes using a stand mixer on medium-low speed. The dough should become smooth, elastic, and slightly tacky.
3. **First Rise (Bulk Fermentation):**
   - Place the kneaded dough in a lightly oiled bowl, cover with plastic wrap or a kitchen towel, and let it rise in a warm, draft-free place for about 1 to 1.5 hours, or until doubled in size.
4. **Shaping and Cutting:**
   - Turn the risen dough out onto a lightly floured surface. Gently deflate the dough and roll it out to about 1/2 inch (1.5 cm) thickness.
   - Using a round cutter or a glass (about 3-4 inches in diameter), cut out rounds of dough. Place them on a baking sheet dusted with cornmeal or semolina flour.
5. **Second Rise:**
   - Cover the cut-out muffins loosely with plastic wrap or a kitchen towel and let them rise again for about 30-45 minutes, or until they puff up and increase slightly in size.
6. **Cooking on the Stove:**
   - Heat a non-stick skillet or griddle over medium-low heat. Lightly grease the skillet with oil or butter.
   - Carefully transfer the risen muffins to the skillet, leaving space between them. Cook for about 5-7 minutes on each side, or until they are golden brown and cooked through. You may need to adjust the heat to ensure they cook evenly without burning.
7. **Baking in the Oven (Optional):**

- If preferred, you can also bake the muffins in a preheated 375°F (190°C) oven for about 10-12 minutes after cooking them on the skillet. This helps ensure they are fully cooked inside.
8. **Cooling:**
    - Transfer the cooked English muffins to a wire rack to cool slightly before splitting them open with a fork. This creates the classic nooks and crannies inside.

Tips:

- **Cornmeal or Semolina Flour:** Dusting the baking sheet with cornmeal or semolina flour prevents the muffins from sticking and adds a nice texture to the bottom.
- **Splitting:** To split the muffins, use a fork to gently pull them apart along the natural seams. This creates nooks and crannies that are perfect for holding butter, jam, or other toppings.
- **Toasting:** Toast the English muffins before serving for the best flavor and texture. They are delicious topped with butter, jam, or used for breakfast sandwiches.

Enjoy your homemade English muffins as a delicious breakfast or snack. Their soft interior and crisp exterior make them a favorite choice for any time of day!

Naan Bread

Ingredients:

- 400g all-purpose flour (about 3 cups)
- 7g instant yeast (about 2 teaspoons)
- 10g granulated sugar (about 2 teaspoons)
- 5g salt (about 1 teaspoon)
- 150ml lukewarm milk (about 2/3 cup)
- 150ml lukewarm water (about 2/3 cup)
- 60ml plain yogurt (about 1/4 cup)
- 2 tablespoons vegetable oil (plus more for greasing)
- Optional toppings: garlic butter, chopped cilantro, nigella seeds, etc.

Instructions:

1. **Activate the Yeast:**
   - In a small bowl, combine the lukewarm milk, lukewarm water, sugar, and instant yeast. Stir well and let it sit for about 5-10 minutes until frothy.
2. **Mixing the Dough:**
   - In a large mixing bowl, combine the all-purpose flour and salt. Make a well in the center and pour in the activated yeast mixture, plain yogurt, and vegetable oil.
   - Mix everything together with a wooden spoon or your hands until a rough dough forms.
3. **Kneading:**
   - Turn the dough out onto a lightly floured surface and knead it for about 8-10 minutes until it becomes smooth, elastic, and slightly tacky. Alternatively, you can knead the dough in a stand mixer fitted with a dough hook for about 5-7 minutes.
4. **First Rise (Proofing):**
   - Place the kneaded dough in a lightly oiled bowl, cover with plastic wrap or a kitchen towel, and let it rise in a warm, draft-free place for about 1 to 1.5 hours, or until doubled in size.
5. **Preheat the Oven:**
   - If you have a pizza stone, place it in the oven and preheat to the highest setting (usually around 500°F/260°C). If not using a pizza stone, preheat a baking sheet in the oven.
6. **Divide and Shape:**
   - Once the dough has risen, punch it down gently to deflate it. Divide the dough into 8 equal portions and shape each portion into a ball.
7. **Roll Out the Naan:**
   - On a lightly floured surface, roll out each ball of dough into an oval or teardrop shape, about 1/4 inch (6mm) thick. You can also stretch the dough gently with your hands to achieve the desired shape.
8. **Bake the Naan:**

- Carefully place the rolled-out naan onto the preheated pizza stone or baking sheet. Bake for 2-3 minutes, or until the naan puffs up and the bottom is golden brown with some charred spots.

9. **Finish:**
   - Remove the naan from the oven and brush immediately with melted garlic butter or plain melted butter. Sprinkle with chopped cilantro, nigella seeds, or any other toppings you prefer.

10. **Serve:**
    - Serve the naan bread warm, either on its own or with your favorite Indian dishes like curries, dal, or grilled meats.

Tips:

- **Cooking Methods:** If you don't have an oven, you can cook naan on a preheated skillet or grill pan over medium-high heat. Cook each side for about 1-2 minutes, or until puffed and charred.
- **Toppings:** Customize your naan with different toppings such as minced garlic, chopped fresh herbs, sesame seeds, or even cheese before baking.
- **Storage:** Naan is best enjoyed fresh and warm. However, you can store leftover naan in an airtight container or sealed plastic bag at room temperature for up to 2 days. Reheat before serving for best results.

Enjoy your homemade naan bread as a delicious accompaniment to your favorite Indian dishes or as a tasty snack on its own!

Garlic Knots

Ingredients:

For the dough:

- 500g bread flour (about 3.5 cups)
- 10g salt (about 2 teaspoons)
- 10g granulated sugar (about 2 teaspoons)
- 7g instant yeast (about 2 teaspoons)
- 30g unsalted butter, softened (about 2 tablespoons)
- 320ml lukewarm water (about 1 and 1/3 cups)

For brushing:

- 60ml olive oil (about 1/4 cup)
- 3-4 cloves garlic, minced
- 2 tablespoons chopped fresh parsley (optional)
- Salt, to taste

Instructions:

1. **Mixing the Dough:**
   - In a large mixing bowl or the bowl of a stand mixer fitted with a dough hook, combine the bread flour, salt, sugar, and instant yeast.
   - Add the softened butter and lukewarm water. Mix until a rough dough forms.
2. **Kneading:**
   - Knead the dough for about 8-10 minutes by hand on a well-floured surface, or 6-8 minutes using a stand mixer on medium-low speed. The dough should become smooth, elastic, and slightly tacky.
3. **First Rise (Bulk Fermentation):**
   - Place the kneaded dough in a lightly oiled bowl, cover with plastic wrap or a kitchen towel, and let it rise in a warm, draft-free place for about 1 to 1.5 hours, or until doubled in size.
4. **Shaping the Knots:**
   - Once the dough has risen, punch it down gently to deflate it. Divide the dough into 16 equal portions.
   - Roll each portion into a rope about 8 inches (20 cm) long.
5. **Forming the Knots:**
   - Tie each rope into a simple knot, tucking the ends underneath. Place the formed knots onto parchment-lined baking sheets, leaving space between them.
6. **Second Rise:**
   - Cover the knots loosely with plastic wrap or a kitchen towel and let them rise again for about 30 minutes to 1 hour, or until they puff up and increase in size.
7. **Baking:**

- Preheat your oven to 375°F (190°C).
- Bake the garlic knots in the preheated oven for 12-15 minutes, or until they are golden brown on top and cooked through.

8. **Preparing the Garlic Oil:**
   - While the knots are baking, heat the olive oil in a small saucepan over medium heat. Add the minced garlic and cook for 1-2 minutes, stirring frequently, until the garlic is fragrant and just starting to turn golden. Remove from heat and stir in the chopped parsley (if using) and salt to taste.
9. **Finishing:**
   - Immediately after removing the knots from the oven, brush them generously with the garlic oil mixture while they are still warm.
10. **Serve:**
    - Serve the garlic knots warm as a delicious appetizer or alongside your favorite pasta dishes.

Tips:

- **Variations:** Feel free to sprinkle grated Parmesan cheese or crushed red pepper flakes over the knots before baking for added flavor.
- **Storage:** Garlic knots are best enjoyed fresh. However, you can store leftover knots in an airtight container at room temperature for up to 2 days. Reheat in the oven briefly before serving to restore their freshness.

Enjoy your homemade garlic knots with their soft, fluffy texture and aromatic garlic-infused oil—a perfect complement to any Italian-inspired meal or as a tasty snack!

Irish Soda Bread

Ingredients:

- 400g all-purpose flour (about 3 cups)
- 100g whole wheat flour (about 3/4 cup) (optional for a slightly heartier texture)
- 1 teaspoon baking soda
- 1 teaspoon salt
- 400ml buttermilk (about 1 and 2/3 cups)
- Optional: 1-2 tablespoons honey or granulated sugar (for a slightly sweeter bread)
- Optional: 50g unsalted butter, melted (about 3.5 tablespoons), for brushing on top

Instructions:

1. **Preheat the Oven:**
   - Preheat your oven to 400°F (200°C). Lightly grease or line a baking sheet with parchment paper.
2. **Mixing the Dry Ingredients:**
   - In a large mixing bowl, whisk together the all-purpose flour, whole wheat flour (if using), baking soda, and salt. If you're adding honey or sugar for sweetness, mix it into the dry ingredients now.
3. **Adding the Buttermilk:**
   - Make a well in the center of the dry ingredients and pour in the buttermilk. Use a wooden spoon or your hands to gently mix the ingredients until a rough dough forms. The dough should be soft and slightly sticky.
4. **Shaping the Dough:**
   - Turn the dough out onto a lightly floured surface. Knead it gently for about 1-2 minutes until it comes together and forms a round loaf. Avoid over-kneading to keep the bread tender.
5. **Baking the Bread:**
   - Place the shaped dough onto the prepared baking sheet. Use a sharp knife to score a deep cross on the top of the loaf, about 1/2 inch (1.5 cm) deep. This helps the bread to bake evenly and allows steam to escape.
   - Bake in the preheated oven for 40-45 minutes, or until the bread is golden brown and sounds hollow when tapped on the bottom.
6. **Finishing:**
   - Optional: Brush the top of the bread with melted butter while it's still warm from the oven. This adds a delicious flavor and helps soften the crust.
7. **Cooling:**
   - Transfer the Irish Soda Bread to a wire rack to cool completely before slicing. This helps to set the crumb and texture.

Tips:

- **Buttermilk Substitute:** If you don't have buttermilk, you can make a substitute by mixing 1 tablespoon of white vinegar or lemon juice with enough milk to make 1 cup (240ml). Let it sit for 5-10 minutes before using.
- **Variations:** You can customize your Irish Soda Bread by adding raisins or currants for a sweeter version, or seeds like caraway or sesame for added flavor and texture.
- **Storage:** Store leftover Irish Soda Bread in an airtight container or wrapped tightly in foil at room temperature for up to 3 days. It's best enjoyed fresh or lightly toasted.

Enjoy your homemade Irish Soda Bread warm with butter, jam, or alongside soups and stews. Its rustic charm and simple preparation make it a favorite for any occasion!

Whole Grain Dinner Rolls

Ingredients:

- 300g whole wheat flour (about 2.5 cups)
- 200g bread flour (about 1.5 cups)
- 10g salt (about 2 teaspoons)
- 10g instant yeast (about 2 teaspoons)
- 30g honey or granulated sugar (about 2 tablespoons)
- 300ml lukewarm water (about 1 and 1/4 cups)
- 60ml olive oil or melted butter (about 1/4 cup)
- Optional: 1 egg (for brushing on top)
- Optional: Seeds (such as sesame, poppy, or sunflower) for topping

Instructions:

1. **Mixing the Dough:**
   - In a large mixing bowl or the bowl of a stand mixer fitted with a dough hook, combine the whole wheat flour, bread flour, salt, instant yeast, and honey or sugar.
   - Add the lukewarm water and olive oil or melted butter. Mix until a rough dough forms.
2. **Kneading:**
   - Knead the dough for about 10-12 minutes by hand on a well-floured surface, or 8-10 minutes using a stand mixer on medium-low speed. The dough should become smooth, elastic, and slightly tacky.
3. **First Rise (Bulk Fermentation):**
   - Place the kneaded dough in a lightly oiled bowl, cover with plastic wrap or a kitchen towel, and let it rise in a warm, draft-free place for about 1 to 1.5 hours, or until doubled in size.
4. **Shaping the Rolls:**
   - Once the dough has risen, gently punch it down to deflate. Turn it out onto a lightly floured surface and divide it into 12 equal portions.
   - Shape each portion into a smooth ball by pulling the edges underneath and pinching to seal at the bottom. Place the shaped rolls onto a parchment-lined baking sheet, leaving space between them.
5. **Second Rise:**
   - Cover the shaped rolls loosely with plastic wrap or a kitchen towel and let them rise again for about 30-45 minutes, or until they have doubled in size.
6. **Preheat the Oven:**
   - About 30 minutes before baking, preheat your oven to 375°F (190°C).
7. **Egg Wash and Topping (Optional):**
   - If desired, beat an egg and brush the tops of the rolls with the egg wash. This gives them a shiny finish after baking.

- Sprinkle seeds or oats on top of the rolls for added texture and flavor.
8. **Baking:**
    - Bake the rolls in the preheated oven for 15-18 minutes, or until they are golden brown on top and sound hollow when tapped on the bottom.
9. **Cooling:**
    - Transfer the baked whole grain dinner rolls to a wire rack to cool slightly before serving. This helps to maintain their texture.

Tips:

- **Variations:** Feel free to customize your whole grain dinner rolls by adding herbs like rosemary or thyme to the dough, or mixing in seeds like flaxseed or chia seeds for added nutrition.
- **Storage:** Store leftover rolls in an airtight container at room temperature for up to 2-3 days. Warm them briefly in the oven before serving to refresh.

These whole grain dinner rolls are perfect for serving alongside soups, salads, or as part of a festive dinner spread. Enjoy their hearty texture and wholesome flavor!

Bagels

Ingredients:

For the dough:

- 500g bread flour (about 4 cups)
- 10g salt (about 2 teaspoons)
- 10g granulated sugar (about 2 teaspoons)
- 7g instant yeast (about 2 teaspoons)
- 300ml lukewarm water (about 1 and 1/4 cups)

For boiling:

- Water, for boiling (about 3-4 quarts)
- 2 tablespoons honey or barley malt syrup (optional, for boiling)

For topping (optional):

- Sesame seeds, poppy seeds, everything bagel seasoning, etc.

Instructions:

1. **Mixing the Dough:**
   - In a large mixing bowl or the bowl of a stand mixer fitted with a dough hook, combine the bread flour, salt, sugar, and instant yeast.
   - Gradually add the lukewarm water while mixing, until a rough dough forms.
2. **Kneading:**
   - Knead the dough for about 10-12 minutes by hand on a well-floured surface, or 8-10 minutes using a stand mixer on medium-low speed. The dough should become smooth, elastic, and slightly tacky.
3. **First Rise (Bulk Fermentation):**
   - Place the kneaded dough in a lightly oiled bowl, cover with plastic wrap or a kitchen towel, and let it rise in a warm, draft-free place for about 1 hour, or until doubled in size.
4. **Shaping the Bagels:**
   - Once the dough has risen, punch it down gently to deflate. Turn it out onto a lightly floured surface and divide it into 8 equal portions.
   - Roll each portion into a smooth ball. To shape each ball into a bagel, flatten it slightly with your palm. Use your thumb to poke a hole through the center, then gently stretch the dough to widen the hole to about 1-2 inches in diameter. The bagel should be about 4-5 inches in diameter overall.
5. **Second Rise:**

- Place the shaped bagels onto a parchment-lined baking sheet, leaving space between them. Cover loosely with plastic wrap or a kitchen towel and let them rise again for about 20-30 minutes. They should puff up slightly.

6. **Boiling the Bagels:**
   - Preheat your oven to 425°F (220°C). Bring a large pot of water to a boil, then reduce the heat to a simmer. Add honey or barley malt syrup to the water if desired (this helps to give the bagels a shiny crust and slightly sweet flavor).
   - Carefully lower 2-3 bagels at a time into the simmering water. Boil for about 1-2 minutes on each side (2-4 minutes total), flipping them once. Use a slotted spoon or skimmer to remove them from the water and place them back onto the parchment-lined baking sheet.

7. **Topping (Optional):**
   - Sprinkle the boiled bagels with sesame seeds, poppy seeds, everything bagel seasoning, or any other toppings you prefer while they are still wet from boiling. This helps the toppings to stick.

8. **Baking:**
   - Bake the bagels in the preheated oven for 20-25 minutes, or until they are golden brown and have a slightly crisp crust.

9. **Cooling:**
   - Transfer the baked bagels to a wire rack to cool completely before slicing and serving. Enjoy them warm or toasted with your favorite spreads or fillings.

Tips:

- **Storage:** Once cooled, store leftover bagels in an airtight container at room temperature for up to 2 days. You can also freeze them for longer storage; just thaw and toast before serving.
- **Variations:** Experiment with different toppings and flavors, such as cinnamon raisin, whole wheat, or jalapeño cheddar, by adding ingredients to the dough during mixing.

Homemade bagels are perfect for breakfast, brunch, or anytime you crave a chewy, satisfying bread. Enjoy the process of making them and savor the delicious results!

Cranberry Walnut Bread

Ingredients:

- 250g bread flour (about 2 cups)
- 100g whole wheat flour (about 3/4 cup)
- 7g instant yeast (about 2 teaspoons)
- 5g salt (about 1 teaspoon)
- 25g honey or granulated sugar (about 2 tablespoons)
- 30g unsalted butter, melted (about 2 tablespoons)
- 200ml lukewarm water (about 3/4 cup)
- 100g dried cranberries (about 3/4 cup)
- 75g chopped walnuts (about 1/2 cup)

Instructions:

1. **Mixing the Dough:**
    - In a large mixing bowl or the bowl of a stand mixer fitted with a dough hook, combine the bread flour, whole wheat flour, instant yeast, salt, honey or sugar, melted butter, and lukewarm water.
    - Mix until a rough dough forms.
2. **Kneading:**
    - Knead the dough for about 8-10 minutes by hand on a well-floured surface, or 6-8 minutes using a stand mixer on medium-low speed. The dough should become smooth, elastic, and slightly tacky.
3. **Incorporating Cranberries and Walnuts:**
    - During the last few minutes of kneading, add the dried cranberries and chopped walnuts to the dough. Knead until they are evenly distributed.
4. **First Rise (Bulk Fermentation):**
    - Place the kneaded dough in a lightly oiled bowl, cover with plastic wrap or a kitchen towel, and let it rise in a warm, draft-free place for about 1 to 1.5 hours, or until doubled in size.
5. **Shaping the Loaf:**
    - Once the dough has risen, gently punch it down to deflate. Turn it out onto a lightly floured surface and shape it into a loaf. You can do this by flattening the dough into a rectangle, then rolling it up tightly from one end and pinching the seam to seal.
6. **Second Rise:**
    - Place the shaped loaf into a greased or parchment-lined loaf pan. Cover loosely with plastic wrap or a kitchen towel and let it rise again for about 30-45 minutes, or until it has risen just above the edges of the pan.
7. **Preheat the Oven:**
    - About 20 minutes before baking, preheat your oven to 375°F (190°C).
8. **Baking:**

- Bake the cranberry walnut bread in the preheated oven for 30-35 minutes, or until the top is golden brown and the loaf sounds hollow when tapped on the bottom.
9. **Cooling:**
    - Remove the bread from the loaf pan and transfer it to a wire rack to cool completely before slicing. This helps to set the crumb and texture.

Tips:

- **Variations:** If you prefer a sweeter bread, you can increase the amount of honey or sugar. You can also add a sprinkle of cinnamon or nutmeg for extra flavor.
- **Storage:** Store leftover cranberry walnut bread in an airtight container at room temperature for up to 3 days. It also freezes well; slice it before freezing for easy individual portions.
- **Serving:** Enjoy slices of cranberry walnut bread plain, toasted with butter, or with cream cheese for a delicious breakfast or snack.

This cranberry walnut bread is sure to be a hit with its sweet-tart cranberries and crunchy walnuts complementing the soft bread crumb. Enjoy baking and savoring this homemade treat!

Pizza Dough

Ingredients:

- 300g bread flour (about 2 cups)
- 5g instant yeast (about 1.5 teaspoons)
- 5g salt (about 1 teaspoon)
- 5g granulated sugar (about 1 teaspoon)
- 200ml lukewarm water (about 3/4 cup)
- 15ml olive oil (about 1 tablespoon)

Instructions:

1. **Mixing the Dough:**
   - In a large mixing bowl or the bowl of a stand mixer fitted with a dough hook, combine the bread flour, instant yeast, salt, and sugar.
   - Make a well in the center and add the lukewarm water and olive oil.
2. **Kneading:**
   - Mix the ingredients together until they form a rough dough. If using a stand mixer, knead on medium-low speed for about 8-10 minutes until the dough is smooth, elastic, and slightly tacky. If kneading by hand, turn the dough out onto a lightly floured surface and knead for about 10-12 minutes.
3. **First Rise (Bulk Fermentation):**
   - Shape the dough into a ball and place it in a lightly oiled bowl, turning once to coat. Cover the bowl with plastic wrap or a kitchen towel and let the dough rise in a warm, draft-free place for about 1 to 1.5 hours, or until doubled in size.
4. **Shaping the Pizza Dough:**
   - Once the dough has risen, punch it down gently to deflate and transfer it to a lightly floured surface. Shape the dough into a round ball and let it rest for 10-15 minutes, covered with a clean kitchen towel or plastic wrap.
5. **Rolling Out the Dough:**
   - Preheat your oven to the highest setting (usually around 500°F/260°C) or as high as your oven will go.
   - Roll out the dough on a lightly floured surface using a rolling pin, starting from the center and working outwards. Roll the dough to your desired thickness, typically about 1/4 inch (6mm) thick for a thin crust pizza.
6. **Topping and Baking:**
   - Transfer the rolled-out dough to a parchment-lined baking sheet or pizza stone.
   - Add your favorite pizza toppings, such as tomato sauce, cheese, vegetables, and meats.
7. **Baking:**
   - Bake the pizza in the preheated oven for about 10-12 minutes, or until the crust is golden brown and the cheese is melted and bubbly.
8. **Cooling and Serving:**

- Remove the pizza from the oven and let it cool slightly before slicing and serving.

Tips:

- **Resting the Dough:** Allowing the dough to rest after shaping and before rolling out helps relax the gluten and makes it easier to stretch or roll out without springing back.
- **Customization:** Customize your pizza dough by adding herbs or spices to the dough during mixing, such as dried oregano, garlic powder, or red pepper flakes.
- **Freezing:** You can freeze pizza dough for later use. Divide the dough into individual portions, wrap each tightly in plastic wrap, and store in a freezer bag for up to 3 months. Thaw in the refrigerator overnight before using.

Enjoy your homemade pizza with your favorite toppings and savor the fresh, crispy crust made from scratch!

Cornbread

Ingredients:

- 1 cup yellow cornmeal
- 1 cup all-purpose flour
- 1/4 cup granulated sugar (adjust to taste for sweeter or less sweet cornbread)
- 1 tablespoon baking powder
- 1/2 teaspoon baking soda
- 1/2 teaspoon salt
- 1 cup buttermilk (or substitute with 1 cup milk + 1 tablespoon vinegar or lemon juice, let sit for 5 minutes)
- 2 large eggs
- 1/2 cup unsalted butter, melted (about 1 stick)
- Optional: 1/2 cup canned corn kernels, drained

Instructions:

1. **Preheat Oven and Prepare Pan:**
   - Preheat your oven to 375°F (190°C). Grease a 9-inch square baking pan or a 10-inch cast iron skillet.
2. **Mix Dry Ingredients:**
   - In a large bowl, whisk together the cornmeal, flour, sugar, baking powder, baking soda, and salt until well combined.
3. **Mix Wet Ingredients:**
   - In another bowl, whisk together the buttermilk, eggs, and melted butter until smooth.
4. **Combine Wet and Dry Ingredients:**
   - Pour the wet ingredients into the bowl with the dry ingredients. Stir gently until just combined. Be careful not to overmix; a few lumps are okay. If using canned corn kernels, gently fold them into the batter.
5. **Bake:**
   - Pour the batter into the prepared baking pan or skillet, spreading it evenly with a spatula.
   - Bake in the preheated oven for 25-30 minutes, or until the top is golden brown and a toothpick inserted into the center comes out clean.
6. **Cool and Serve:**
   - Remove from the oven and let the cornbread cool in the pan for 10 minutes before slicing and serving.

Tips:

- **Variations:** For a savory twist, add chopped jalapeños, shredded cheese, or cooked bacon to the batter.

- **Storage:** Store leftover cornbread tightly wrapped or in an airtight container at room temperature for up to 3 days. It can also be frozen for longer storage; wrap slices individually and thaw before reheating.
- **Serve with:** Enjoy cornbread warm with butter, honey, or alongside your favorite chili, soup, or barbecue dishes.

Homemade cornbread is a comforting and delicious addition to any meal. Its versatility and simple preparation make it a beloved staple in many households. Enjoy baking and savoring this Southern favorite!

Swedish Limpa Bread

Ingredients:

- 1 cup lukewarm water (about 240ml)
- 1/2 cup molasses
- 1/4 cup orange juice
- 2 tablespoons unsalted butter, melted
- 2 teaspoons active dry yeast
- 2 teaspoons finely grated orange zest
- 1 teaspoon ground anise or fennel seeds (optional)
- 1 teaspoon salt
- 1 cup rye flour
- 2 cups bread flour (or all-purpose flour)
- Cornmeal, for dusting

Instructions:

1. **Activate Yeast:**
   - In a small bowl, combine the lukewarm water, molasses, and orange juice. Sprinkle the yeast over the mixture and let it sit for about 5-10 minutes until foamy.
2. **Mix Wet Ingredients:**
   - Stir in the melted butter, orange zest, ground anise or fennel seeds (if using), and salt into the yeast mixture.
3. **Combine Flours:**
   - In a large mixing bowl, combine the rye flour and bread (or all-purpose) flour.
4. **Mix Dough:**
   - Gradually add the wet ingredients to the flour mixture, stirring until the dough comes together. It will be slightly sticky.
5. **Knead:**
   - Turn the dough out onto a lightly floured surface and knead for about 8-10 minutes, or until smooth and elastic. Alternatively, knead using a stand mixer fitted with a dough hook on medium speed for about 5-7 minutes.
6. **First Rise (Bulk Fermentation):**
   - Place the kneaded dough in a lightly oiled bowl, turning once to coat. Cover with plastic wrap or a kitchen towel and let it rise in a warm, draft-free place for about 1 to 1.5 hours, or until doubled in size.
7. **Shape the Loaf:**
   - Punch down the risen dough gently to deflate. Shape it into a round or oval loaf and place it on a baking sheet dusted with cornmeal.
8. **Second Rise:**
   - Cover the shaped loaf loosely with plastic wrap or a kitchen towel and let it rise again for about 30-45 minutes, or until puffed up.

9. **Preheat Oven:**
    - About 20 minutes before baking, preheat your oven to 375°F (190°C).
10. **Bake:**
    - Bake the Swedish Limpa Bread in the preheated oven for 30-35 minutes, or until it is golden brown and sounds hollow when tapped on the bottom.
11. **Cool:**
    - Transfer the baked bread to a wire rack to cool completely before slicing.

Tips:

- **Flavor Variations:** Experiment with the spices to your liking. Some recipes use caraway seeds instead of anise or fennel, and some may include a touch of ground cloves or ginger for extra depth.
- **Storage:** Store the cooled Swedish Limpa Bread in an airtight container or wrapped tightly in foil at room temperature for up to 3 days. It can also be frozen for longer storage; slice it before freezing for easy thawing and reheating.

Enjoy your homemade Swedish Limpa Bread with butter, cheese, or as part of a traditional Swedish meal. Its rich flavor and aroma make it a delightful treat any time of day!

Portuguese Sweet Bread

Ingredients:

- 4 cups all-purpose flour
- 1/2 cup granulated sugar
- 1 teaspoon salt
- 2 and 1/4 teaspoons active dry yeast (1 packet)
- 1/2 cup whole milk, lukewarm
- 1/4 cup unsalted butter, melted and cooled
- 3 large eggs, at room temperature
- 1/4 cup water, lukewarm
- Zest of 1 lemon or orange (optional, for flavor)
- 1 egg yolk + 1 tablespoon milk (for egg wash)
- Optional: 1/2 teaspoon vanilla extract or lemon extract for added flavor

Instructions:

1. **Activate Yeast:**
    - In a small bowl, dissolve 1 teaspoon of sugar in the lukewarm milk. Sprinkle the yeast over the milk mixture and let it sit for about 5-10 minutes until frothy.
2. **Mix Dough:**
    - In a large mixing bowl or the bowl of a stand mixer fitted with a dough hook, combine the flour, remaining sugar, and salt. Add the melted butter, eggs, water, and activated yeast mixture (and optional vanilla or lemon extract). Mix until a rough dough forms.
3. **Knead:**
    - Knead the dough for about 10-12 minutes by hand on a well-floured surface, or 8-10 minutes using a stand mixer on medium-low speed. The dough should become smooth, elastic, and slightly tacky.
4. **First Rise (Bulk Fermentation):**
    - Place the kneaded dough in a lightly oiled bowl, turning once to coat. Cover with plastic wrap or a kitchen towel and let it rise in a warm, draft-free place for about 1 to 1.5 hours, or until doubled in size.
5. **Shape the Loaf:**
    - Punch down the risen dough gently to deflate. Turn it out onto a lightly floured surface and shape it into a round or oval loaf. Place it on a parchment-lined baking sheet.
6. **Second Rise:**
    - Cover the shaped loaf loosely with plastic wrap or a kitchen towel and let it rise again for about 30-45 minutes, or until puffed up.
7. **Preheat Oven:**
    - About 20 minutes before baking, preheat your oven to 350°F (175°C).
8. **Egg Wash:**

- In a small bowl, whisk together the egg yolk and tablespoon of milk. Brush the top of the risen loaf with the egg wash.
9. **Bake:**
    - Bake the Portuguese Sweet Bread in the preheated oven for 30-35 minutes, or until it is golden brown on top and sounds hollow when tapped on the bottom.
10. **Cool:**
    - Transfer the baked bread to a wire rack to cool completely before slicing.

Tips:

- **Flavor Variations:** You can customize the flavor by adding zest of lemon or orange to the dough for a citrusy note, or even sprinkle the top with pearl sugar before baking for extra sweetness and crunch.
- **Storage:** Store the cooled Portuguese Sweet Bread in an airtight container or wrapped tightly in foil at room temperature for up to 3 days. It can also be frozen for longer storage; slice it before freezing for easy thawing and reheating.

Enjoy your homemade Portuguese Sweet Bread with butter, jam, or as part of a festive meal. Its tender texture and subtle sweetness make it a delightful treat any time of day!

Parker House Rolls

Ingredients:

- 4 cups all-purpose flour
- 1/4 cup granulated sugar
- 2 and 1/4 teaspoons active dry yeast (1 packet)
- 1 and 1/4 cups whole milk, lukewarm
- 1/2 cup unsalted butter, melted and cooled (plus extra for brushing)
- 1 large egg, at room temperature
- 1 teaspoon salt
- Optional: Flaky sea salt for sprinkling on top

Instructions:

1. **Activate Yeast:**
    - In a small bowl, dissolve 1 teaspoon of sugar in the lukewarm milk. Sprinkle the yeast over the milk mixture and let it sit for about 5-10 minutes until frothy.
2. **Mix Dough:**
    - In a large mixing bowl or the bowl of a stand mixer fitted with a dough hook, combine the flour, remaining sugar, and salt. Add the melted butter, activated yeast mixture, and egg. Mix until a soft dough forms.
3. **Knead:**
    - Knead the dough for about 8-10 minutes by hand on a well-floured surface, or 6-8 minutes using a stand mixer on medium-low speed. The dough should be smooth, elastic, and slightly tacky.
4. **First Rise (Bulk Fermentation):**
    - Place the kneaded dough in a lightly oiled bowl, turning once to coat. Cover with plastic wrap or a kitchen towel and let it rise in a warm, draft-free place for about 1 to 1.5 hours, or until doubled in size.
5. **Shaping the Rolls:**
    - Punch down the risen dough gently to deflate. Turn it out onto a lightly floured surface and divide it into 16 equal pieces.
6. **Forming the Rolls:**
    - Roll each piece of dough into a ball. Using a rolling pin, flatten each ball into an oval or rectangle shape, about 1/4 inch (6mm) thick.
7. **Folding:**
    - Brush each flattened dough piece generously with melted butter. Fold the dough in half over itself to create a half-moon shape, gently pressing the edges to seal.
8. **Second Rise:**
    - Place the folded rolls onto a parchment-lined baking sheet, spacing them slightly apart. Cover loosely with plastic wrap or a kitchen towel and let them rise again for about 30-45 minutes, or until puffed up.
9. **Preheat Oven:**

- About 20 minutes before baking, preheat your oven to 375°F (190°C).
10. **Bake:**
    - Bake the Parker House Rolls in the preheated oven for 15-18 minutes, or until they are golden brown on top and sound hollow when tapped on the bottom.
11. **Cool and Serve:**
    - Remove the rolls from the oven and immediately brush the tops with more melted butter. Sprinkle with flaky sea salt if desired. Transfer to a wire rack to cool slightly before serving.

Tips:

- **Make-Ahead:** You can make the dough ahead of time and refrigerate it overnight after the first rise. Let it come to room temperature before shaping and proceeding with the recipe.
- **Storage:** Store leftover Parker House Rolls in an airtight container at room temperature for up to 3 days. They can also be frozen for longer storage; thaw and reheat before serving.

These Parker House Rolls are perfect for serving alongside meals or as part of a festive dinner spread. Enjoy their soft, buttery goodness straight from the oven!

Cheese Bread

Ingredients:

- 1 cup whole milk
- 1/2 cup unsalted butter (1 stick)
- 1 teaspoon salt
- 2 cups tapioca flour (also known as tapioca starch)
- 2/3 cup grated Parmesan cheese
- 2/3 cup grated mozzarella cheese
- 2 large eggs, beaten

Instructions:

1. **Preheat Oven:**
    - Preheat your oven to 375°F (190°C). Grease a mini muffin tin or line with mini muffin liners.
2. **Prepare the Batter:**
    - In a saucepan, combine the milk, butter, and salt. Heat over medium heat until the butter is melted and the mixture just starts to simmer (do not boil).
3. **Add Tapioca Flour:**
    - Remove from heat and add the tapioca flour all at once. Stir vigorously until the mixture comes together into a smooth dough-like consistency.
4. **Cool the Mixture:**
    - Transfer the mixture to a mixing bowl and let it cool for about 5-10 minutes, until it is cool enough to handle but still warm.
5. **Add Cheese and Eggs:**
    - Gradually add the grated Parmesan and mozzarella cheeses to the dough, mixing well after each addition. The mixture will be thick.
    - Add the beaten eggs to the dough, a little at a time, mixing well after each addition until fully incorporated. The dough will be sticky.
6. **Shape and Bake:**
    - Using a small cookie scoop or spoon, portion the dough into the prepared mini muffin tin, filling each cup nearly to the top.
7. **Bake:**
    - Bake in the preheated oven for 15-20 minutes, or until the cheese bread puffs up and the tops are lightly golden brown.
8. **Cool and Serve:**
    - Remove the cheese bread from the muffin tin and let them cool slightly on a wire rack. Serve warm.

Tips:

- **Cheese Variations:** Feel free to experiment with different cheeses such as cheddar, Gouda, or a combination of your favorites.
- **Storage:** Store leftover cheese bread in an airtight container at room temperature for up to 2 days. Reheat in the oven or microwave before serving to regain their soft texture.

Enjoy these Brazilian cheese bread (Pão de Queijo) as a delicious appetizer, snack, or side dish. Their cheesy, chewy texture makes them irresistible!

Olive Bread

Ingredients:

- 3 cups all-purpose flour
- 1 and 1/2 teaspoons instant yeast
- 1 teaspoon salt
- 1 cup warm water
- 2 tablespoons olive oil
- 1 cup chopped mixed olives (such as Kalamata and green olives)
- 1/2 cup grated Parmesan cheese (optional, for added flavor)

Instructions:

1. **Mixing the Dough:**
    - In a large mixing bowl, combine the flour, instant yeast, and salt.
    - Make a well in the center and add the warm water and olive oil.
    - Stir until the dough comes together.
2. **Kneading:**
    - Turn the dough out onto a lightly floured surface and knead for about 8-10 minutes, or until the dough is smooth and elastic. Alternatively, knead using a stand mixer fitted with a dough hook for about 5-7 minutes on medium-low speed.
3. **First Rise (Bulk Fermentation):**
    - Place the kneaded dough in a lightly oiled bowl, turning once to coat. Cover with plastic wrap or a kitchen towel and let it rise in a warm, draft-free place for about 1 to 1.5 hours, or until doubled in size.
4. **Adding Olives:**
    - Once the dough has risen, gently punch it down to deflate. Fold in the chopped olives and grated Parmesan cheese, if using, until evenly distributed throughout the dough.
5. **Shaping:**
    - Shape the dough into a round or oval loaf and place it on a parchment-lined baking sheet.
6. **Second Rise:**
    - Cover the shaped loaf loosely with plastic wrap or a kitchen towel and let it rise again for about 30-45 minutes, or until puffed up.
7. **Preheat Oven:**
    - About 20 minutes before baking, preheat your oven to 375°F (190°C).
8. **Baking:**
    - Bake the olive bread in the preheated oven for 30-35 minutes, or until it is golden brown on top and sounds hollow when tapped on the bottom.
9. **Cooling:**
    - Transfer the baked olive bread to a wire rack to cool completely before slicing.

Tips:

- **Variations:** You can add herbs like rosemary or thyme to enhance the flavor of the olive bread. Adjust the amount of olives to your preference for a more or less pronounced olive flavor.
- **Storage:** Store leftover olive bread in an airtight container at room temperature for up to 3 days. It can also be frozen; slice it before freezing for easier reheating.

Enjoy your homemade olive bread with soups, salads, or as a delicious snack on its own. The combination of olives and bread makes it a wonderful addition to any meal!

Sunflower Seed Bread

Ingredients:

- 1 and 1/2 cups warm water (about 110°F/45°C)
- 2 teaspoons active dry yeast
- 1 tablespoon honey or sugar
- 3 cups bread flour
- 1 cup whole wheat flour
- 1/2 cup sunflower seeds (plus extra for topping)
- 1/4 cup flaxseeds (optional)
- 1/4 cup rolled oats
- 2 tablespoons olive oil or melted butter
- 1 and 1/2 teaspoons salt

Instructions:

1. **Activate Yeast:**
    - In a small bowl, combine the warm water, yeast, and honey (or sugar). Stir briefly and let it sit for about 5-10 minutes until the yeast is foamy.
2. **Mixing Dough:**
    - In a large mixing bowl or the bowl of a stand mixer fitted with a dough hook, combine the bread flour, whole wheat flour, sunflower seeds, flaxseeds (if using), rolled oats, and salt.
    - Add the activated yeast mixture and olive oil (or melted butter) to the flour mixture.
3. **Kneading:**
    - Mix the ingredients until a dough forms. Knead the dough for about 8-10 minutes by hand on a lightly floured surface, or 6-8 minutes using a stand mixer on medium-low speed. The dough should be smooth, elastic, and slightly tacky.
4. **First Rise (Bulk Fermentation):**
    - Place the kneaded dough in a lightly oiled bowl, turning once to coat. Cover with plastic wrap or a kitchen towel and let it rise in a warm, draft-free place for about 1 to 1.5 hours, or until doubled in size.
5. **Shaping and Second Rise:**
    - Punch down the risen dough gently to deflate. Shape it into a loaf and place it in a greased 9x5-inch loaf pan. Alternatively, shape the dough into a round or oval loaf and place it on a parchment-lined baking sheet.
    - Cover loosely with plastic wrap or a kitchen towel and let it rise again for about 30-45 minutes, or until puffed up.
6. **Preheat Oven:**
    - About 20 minutes before baking, preheat your oven to 375°F (190°C).
7. **Baking:**

- Brush the top of the loaf with water and sprinkle with additional sunflower seeds if desired.
- Bake in the preheated oven for 30-35 minutes (for a loaf) or 25-30 minutes (for a free-form loaf), or until the bread is golden brown on top and sounds hollow when tapped on the bottom.

8. **Cooling:**
    - Remove the bread from the pan or baking sheet and transfer it to a wire rack to cool completely before slicing.

Tips:

- **Variations:** You can customize this bread by adding other seeds such as pumpkin seeds or sesame seeds. Adjust the amount of seeds according to your preference.
- **Storage:** Store leftover sunflower seed bread in an airtight container at room temperature for up to 3 days. It can also be frozen for longer storage; slice it before freezing for easier reheating.

Enjoy your homemade sunflower seed bread toasted with butter, as a sandwich bread, or alongside soups and salads. Its nutty flavor and wholesome texture make it a delightful addition to any meal!

Pita Bread

Ingredients:

- 3 cups all-purpose flour (plus extra for dusting)
- 1 teaspoon salt
- 1 tablespoon granulated sugar
- 2 teaspoons instant yeast
- 1 and 1/4 cups lukewarm water
- 2 tablespoons olive oil (plus extra for brushing)

Instructions:

1. **Activate Yeast:**
   - In a small bowl, combine the lukewarm water, sugar, and yeast. Stir briefly and let it sit for about 5-10 minutes until the yeast is foamy.
2. **Mixing Dough:**
   - In a large mixing bowl or the bowl of a stand mixer fitted with a dough hook, combine the flour and salt.
   - Add the activated yeast mixture and olive oil to the flour mixture.
3. **Kneading:**
   - Mix the ingredients until a dough forms. Knead the dough for about 8-10 minutes by hand on a lightly floured surface, or 6-8 minutes using a stand mixer on medium-low speed. The dough should be smooth, elastic, and slightly tacky.
4. **First Rise (Bulk Fermentation):**
   - Place the kneaded dough in a lightly oiled bowl, turning once to coat. Cover with plastic wrap or a kitchen towel and let it rise in a warm, draft-free place for about 1 to 1.5 hours, or until doubled in size.
5. **Divide and Shape:**
   - Punch down the risen dough gently to deflate. Divide the dough into 8 equal portions and shape each portion into a ball.
6. **Second Rise:**
   - Cover the dough balls loosely with plastic wrap or a kitchen towel and let them rest for about 15-20 minutes.
7. **Preheat Oven:**
   - While the dough balls are resting, preheat your oven to 475°F (245°C). Place a baking sheet or a pizza stone in the oven to preheat as well.
8. **Roll Out the Dough:**
   - On a lightly floured surface, roll out each dough ball into a circle about 6-8 inches in diameter and 1/4 inch thick. If necessary, you can gently stretch the dough to achieve the desired size and thickness.
9. **Bake the Pita Bread:**

- Carefully place 2-3 rolled-out dough circles onto the preheated baking sheet or pizza stone. Bake for 3-4 minutes, or until puffed up and lightly golden brown. The pita bread should puff up like a balloon.
10. **Cool and Serve:**
    - Remove the baked pita bread from the oven and transfer them to a wire rack to cool slightly. Brush lightly with olive oil if desired.
11. **Repeat:**
    - Continue rolling out and baking the remaining dough balls in batches until all the pita breads are baked.

Tips:

- **Storage:** Pita bread is best served fresh and warm. However, you can store leftover pita bread in an airtight container at room temperature for 1-2 days. To reheat, wrap them in foil and warm in a 350°F (175°C) oven for a few minutes.
- **Variations:** For whole wheat pita bread, substitute up to half of the all-purpose flour with whole wheat flour. You can also sprinkle sesame seeds or za'atar on top of the rolled-out dough before baking for added flavor.

Enjoy your homemade pita bread stuffed with falafel, gyros, or your favorite fillings, or simply use it to scoop up hummus or other dips. Its versatility makes it a staple in many cuisines!

Whole Wheat Challah

Ingredients:

- 1 and 1/2 cups warm water
- 2 and 1/4 teaspoons active dry yeast (1 packet)
- 1/4 cup honey or maple syrup
- 4 tablespoons olive oil or vegetable oil
- 2 large eggs (plus 1 additional egg for egg wash)
- 4 cups whole wheat flour
- 2 cups all-purpose flour (plus extra for dusting)
- 1 and 1/2 teaspoons salt
- Optional: Sesame seeds or poppy seeds for topping

Instructions:

1. **Activate Yeast:**
   - In a large mixing bowl or the bowl of a stand mixer, combine the warm water, honey (or maple syrup), and yeast. Stir briefly and let it sit for about 5-10 minutes until the yeast is foamy.
2. **Mix Wet Ingredients:**
   - Add the olive oil and 2 eggs to the yeast mixture. Stir well to combine.
3. **Add Flours and Salt:**
   - Gradually add the whole wheat flour, all-purpose flour, and salt to the wet ingredients. Mix until a dough forms.
4. **Kneading:**
   - Turn the dough out onto a lightly floured surface and knead for about 10-12 minutes, or until the dough is smooth and elastic. Alternatively, knead using a stand mixer fitted with a dough hook on medium speed for about 8-10 minutes.
5. **First Rise (Bulk Fermentation):**
   - Place the kneaded dough in a lightly oiled bowl, turning once to coat. Cover with plastic wrap or a kitchen towel and let it rise in a warm, draft-free place for about 1 to 1.5 hours, or until doubled in size.
6. **Shape the Challah:**
   - After the dough has risen, punch it down gently to deflate. Divide the dough into three equal portions for a three-strand braid, or six portions for a six-strand braid.
   - Roll each portion into a long rope about 12-14 inches long. Braid the ropes together, pinching the ends together and tucking them under to form a loaf.
7. **Second Rise:**
   - Place the braided challah on a parchment-lined baking sheet. Cover loosely with plastic wrap or a kitchen towel and let it rise again for about 30-45 minutes, or until puffed up.
8. **Preheat Oven:**
   - About 20 minutes before baking, preheat your oven to 350°F (175°C).

9. **Egg Wash and Topping:**
   - In a small bowl, beat the remaining egg. Brush the entire surface of the risen challah with the egg wash. Sprinkle with sesame seeds or poppy seeds if desired.
10. **Bake:**
    - Bake the whole wheat challah in the preheated oven for 30-35 minutes, or until it is golden brown on top and sounds hollow when tapped on the bottom.
11. **Cool and Serve:**
    - Transfer the baked challah to a wire rack to cool completely before slicing.

Tips:

- **Variations:** Feel free to customize your whole wheat challah by adding raisins, dried fruits, or nuts to the dough for extra flavor and texture.
- **Storage:** Store leftover challah in an airtight container or wrapped tightly in foil at room temperature for up to 3 days. It can also be frozen for longer storage; slice it before freezing for easier reheating.

Enjoy your homemade whole wheat challah as part of a Sabbath meal, holiday celebration, or any time you crave a delicious and comforting bread. Its rich flavor and beautiful braided appearance make it a centerpiece at any table!

Honey Oat Bread

Ingredients:

- 1 cup old-fashioned oats
- 1 and 1/2 cups boiling water
- 1/4 cup honey
- 2 tablespoons unsalted butter, softened
- 2 teaspoons salt
- 2 and 1/4 teaspoons active dry yeast (1 packet)
- 1/2 cup warm water (about 110°F/45°C)
- 4 cups bread flour (plus extra for kneading)
- Optional: 1/4 cup whole wheat flour (for added texture)
- Optional: Rolled oats for sprinkling on top

Instructions:

1. **Prepare Oats:**
   - In a heatproof bowl, combine the old-fashioned oats and boiling water. Let it sit for about 10-15 minutes, stirring occasionally, until the oats have absorbed the water and softened. Allow the mixture to cool to lukewarm.
2. **Activate Yeast:**
   - In a small bowl, combine the warm water and honey. Sprinkle the yeast over the mixture and let it sit for about 5-10 minutes until frothy.
3. **Mix Dough:**
   - In a large mixing bowl or the bowl of a stand mixer fitted with a dough hook, combine the softened butter, salt, bread flour, and optional whole wheat flour. Add the cooled oat mixture and the activated yeast mixture.
4. **Kneading:**
   - Mix the ingredients until a dough forms. Knead the dough for about 8-10 minutes by hand on a lightly floured surface, or 6-8 minutes using a stand mixer on medium-low speed. The dough should be smooth, elastic, and slightly tacky.
5. **First Rise (Bulk Fermentation):**
   - Place the kneaded dough in a lightly oiled bowl, turning once to coat. Cover with plastic wrap or a kitchen towel and let it rise in a warm, draft-free place for about 1 to 1.5 hours, or until doubled in size.
6. **Shaping:**
   - After the dough has risen, punch it down gently to deflate. Shape it into a loaf and place it in a greased 9x5-inch loaf pan. Alternatively, shape the dough into a round or oval loaf and place it on a parchment-lined baking sheet.
7. **Second Rise:**
   - Cover the loaf loosely with plastic wrap or a kitchen towel and let it rise again for about 30-45 minutes, or until puffed up.
8. **Preheat Oven:**

- About 20 minutes before baking, preheat your oven to 350°F (175°C).
9. **Bake:**
    - If desired, brush the top of the loaf with water and sprinkle with rolled oats.
    - Bake the honey oat bread in the preheated oven for 30-35 minutes (for a loaf) or 25-30 minutes (for a free-form loaf), or until it is golden brown on top and sounds hollow when tapped on the bottom.
10. **Cool and Serve:**
    - Remove the bread from the pan or baking sheet and transfer it to a wire rack to cool completely before slicing.

Tips:

- **Variations:** You can add nuts, seeds, or dried fruits to the dough for extra flavor and texture.
- **Storage:** Store leftover honey oat bread in an airtight container at room temperature for up to 3 days. It can also be frozen for longer storage; slice it before freezing for easier reheating.

Enjoy your homemade honey oat bread toasted with butter, served with soups, or simply enjoyed on its own. Its hearty texture and subtle sweetness make it a delightful treat for any occasion!

Pretzel Rolls

Ingredients:

For the Dough:

- 1 and 1/2 cups warm water (about 110°F/45°C)
- 1 tablespoon granulated sugar
- 2 and 1/4 teaspoons (1 packet) active dry yeast
- 4 cups bread flour (plus extra for dusting)
- 1 teaspoon salt
- 2 tablespoons unsalted butter, melted
- Optional: 1/4 cup baking soda (for boiling)
- Optional: Coarse salt or pretzel salt for topping

For Boiling:

- 10 cups water
- 1/4 cup baking soda

Instructions:

1. **Activate Yeast:**
   - In a small bowl, combine the warm water and sugar. Sprinkle the yeast over the mixture and let it sit for about 5-10 minutes until frothy.
2. **Mix Dough:**
   - In a large mixing bowl or the bowl of a stand mixer fitted with a dough hook, combine the bread flour and salt. Add the melted butter and activated yeast mixture.
3. **Kneading:**
   - Mix the ingredients until a dough forms. Knead the dough for about 8-10 minutes by hand on a lightly floured surface, or 6-8 minutes using a stand mixer on medium-low speed. The dough should be smooth, elastic, and slightly tacky.
4. **First Rise (Bulk Fermentation):**
   - Place the kneaded dough in a lightly oiled bowl, turning once to coat. Cover with plastic wrap or a kitchen towel and let it rise in a warm, draft-free place for about 1 hour, or until doubled in size.
5. **Shaping:**
   - After the dough has risen, punch it down gently to deflate. Divide the dough into 8-10 equal portions and shape each portion into a smooth ball. Place the balls on a parchment-lined baking sheet, spaced a few inches apart.
6. **Second Rise:**
   - Cover the shaped rolls loosely with plastic wrap or a kitchen towel and let them rise again for about 30-45 minutes, or until puffed up.
7. **Preheat Oven:**

- About 20 minutes before baking, preheat your oven to 425°F (220°C).
8. **Boiling (Optional Step for Traditional Pretzel Texture):**
    - In a large pot, bring 10 cups of water to a boil. Carefully add the baking soda (it will fizz up) and reduce the heat to medium-low.
    - Gently lower a few rolls at a time into the simmering water, using a slotted spoon or spider strainer. Boil each roll for about 30 seconds on each side. Transfer the boiled rolls back to the baking sheet using the slotted spoon.
9. **Baking:**
    - If you skipped boiling, proceed directly to baking. If you boiled the rolls, after boiling, brush each roll with a beaten egg wash (1 egg beaten with 1 tablespoon of water) and sprinkle with coarse salt or pretzel salt.
    - Bake the rolls in the preheated oven for 15-18 minutes, or until they are deeply golden brown and sound hollow when tapped on the bottom.
10. **Cool and Serve:**
    - Transfer the baked pretzel rolls to a wire rack to cool slightly before serving.

Tips:

- **Topping Variations:** Besides coarse salt or pretzel salt, you can experiment with toppings like sesame seeds, poppy seeds, or even grated cheese for added flavor.
- **Storage:** Store leftover pretzel rolls in an airtight container at room temperature for up to 3 days. They can also be frozen; reheat in the oven to regain their crisp crust.

Enjoy your homemade pretzel rolls warm with butter, as sandwich buns, or as a delightful addition to any meal. Their chewy texture and salty exterior make them irresistible!

Rosemary Olive Oil Bread

Ingredients:

- 4 cups bread flour (plus extra for dusting)
- 2 and 1/4 teaspoons (1 packet) active dry yeast
- 1 and 1/2 teaspoons salt
- 1 tablespoon granulated sugar
- 1 and 1/2 cups warm water (about 110°F/45°C)
- 1/4 cup extra virgin olive oil
- 2 tablespoons fresh rosemary, finely chopped (plus extra for topping)
- Optional: Coarse sea salt for topping

Instructions:

1. **Activate Yeast:**
   - In a small bowl, combine the warm water and sugar. Sprinkle the yeast over the mixture and let it sit for about 5-10 minutes until frothy.
2. **Mix Dough:**
   - In a large mixing bowl or the bowl of a stand mixer fitted with a dough hook, combine the bread flour and salt.
   - Add the activated yeast mixture, olive oil, and chopped rosemary to the flour mixture.
3. **Kneading:**
   - Mix the ingredients until a dough forms. Knead the dough for about 8-10 minutes by hand on a lightly floured surface, or 6-8 minutes using a stand mixer on medium-low speed. The dough should be smooth, elastic, and slightly tacky.
4. **First Rise (Bulk Fermentation):**
   - Place the kneaded dough in a lightly oiled bowl, turning once to coat. Cover with plastic wrap or a kitchen towel and let it rise in a warm, draft-free place for about 1 to 1.5 hours, or until doubled in size.
5. **Shaping:**
   - After the dough has risen, punch it down gently to deflate. Shape it into a round or oval loaf and place it on a parchment-lined baking sheet.
6. **Second Rise:**
   - Cover the shaped loaf loosely with plastic wrap or a kitchen towel and let it rise again for about 30-45 minutes, or until puffed up.
7. **Preheat Oven:**
   - About 20 minutes before baking, preheat your oven to 400°F (200°C).
8. **Topping:**
   - Brush the top of the risen loaf with olive oil. Sprinkle with additional chopped rosemary and coarse sea salt if desired.
9. **Bake:**

- Bake the rosemary olive oil bread in the preheated oven for 30-35 minutes, or until it is golden brown on top and sounds hollow when tapped on the bottom.
10. **Cool and Serve:**
    - Transfer the baked bread to a wire rack to cool completely before slicing.

Tips:

- **Variations:** You can add grated Parmesan cheese or olives to the dough for additional flavor variations.
- **Storage:** Store leftover rosemary olive oil bread in an airtight container at room temperature for up to 3 days. It can also be frozen for longer storage; slice it before freezing for easier reheating.

Enjoy your homemade rosemary olive oil bread as a side to soups and salads, or simply toasted with butter. Its aromatic flavor and tender texture make it a delightful addition to any meal!

Raisin Bread

Ingredients:

- 1 cup warm milk (about 110°F/45°C)
- 2 tablespoons unsalted butter, melted
- 1/4 cup granulated sugar
- 2 and 1/4 teaspoons (1 packet) active dry yeast
- 3 cups bread flour (plus extra for kneading)
- 1 teaspoon salt
- 1 cup raisins
- 1/2 teaspoon ground cinnamon (optional, for added flavor)
- 1 large egg, beaten (for egg wash)

Instructions:

1. **Activate Yeast:**
   - In a small bowl, combine the warm milk, melted butter, and sugar. Sprinkle the yeast over the mixture and let it sit for about 5-10 minutes until frothy.
2. **Mix Dough:**
   - In a large mixing bowl or the bowl of a stand mixer fitted with a dough hook, combine the bread flour and salt.
   - Add the activated yeast mixture to the flour mixture and mix until a dough starts to form.
3. **Kneading:**
   - Turn the dough out onto a lightly floured surface and knead for about 8-10 minutes, or until the dough is smooth and elastic. Alternatively, knead using a stand mixer on medium-low speed for 6-8 minutes.
4. **Adding Raisins:**
   - Flatten the kneaded dough and sprinkle the raisins (and ground cinnamon, if using) evenly over the surface.
   - Fold the dough over itself and knead gently to distribute the raisins throughout the dough.
5. **First Rise (Bulk Fermentation):**
   - Place the kneaded dough in a lightly oiled bowl, turning once to coat. Cover with plastic wrap or a kitchen towel and let it rise in a warm, draft-free place for about 1 to 1.5 hours, or until doubled in size.
6. **Shaping:**
   - After the dough has risen, punch it down gently to deflate. Divide the dough into two equal portions and shape each portion into a loaf. Place the loaves in greased 9x5-inch loaf pans.
7. **Second Rise:**
   - Cover the loaf pans loosely with plastic wrap or a kitchen towel and let them rise again for about 30-45 minutes, or until puffed up and nearly doubled in size.

8. **Preheat Oven:**
   - About 20 minutes before baking, preheat your oven to 375°F (190°C).
9. **Egg Wash:**
   - Brush the top of each risen loaf with beaten egg.
10. **Bake:**
    - Bake the raisin bread in the preheated oven for 25-30 minutes, or until the loaves are golden brown on top and sound hollow when tapped on the bottom.
11. **Cool and Serve:**
    - Remove the baked raisin bread from the loaf pans and transfer them to a wire rack to cool completely before slicing.

Tips:

- **Variations:** You can add chopped nuts (such as walnuts or pecans) or dried fruits (such as cranberries or apricots) to the dough for different flavor combinations.
- **Storage:** Store leftover raisin bread in an airtight container or wrapped tightly in foil at room temperature for up to 3 days. It can also be frozen; slice it before freezing for easier reheating.

Enjoy your homemade raisin bread toasted for breakfast, served with afternoon tea, or as a comforting treat any time of the day!

Anadama Bread

Ingredients:

- 1 and 1/2 cups warm water (about 110°F/45°C)
- 1/2 cup cornmeal
- 1/4 cup unsalted butter
- 1/4 cup molasses
- 2 teaspoons salt
- 1 tablespoon active dry yeast
- 4 cups bread flour (plus extra for kneading)
- Optional: Cornmeal for dusting

Instructions:

1. **Prepare Cornmeal Mixture:**
    - In a small saucepan, combine the warm water and cornmeal. Cook over medium heat, stirring constantly, until the mixture thickens (about 3-5 minutes). Remove from heat and stir in the butter, molasses, and salt. Let the mixture cool to lukewarm.
2. **Activate Yeast:**
    - In a small bowl, combine 1/2 cup of the cooled cornmeal mixture with the active dry yeast. Let it sit for about 5-10 minutes until frothy.
3. **Mix Dough:**
    - In a large mixing bowl or the bowl of a stand mixer fitted with a dough hook, combine the bread flour and the remaining cornmeal mixture. Add the activated yeast mixture and mix until a dough forms.
4. **Kneading:**
    - Turn the dough out onto a lightly floured surface and knead for about 8-10 minutes, or until the dough is smooth and elastic. Alternatively, knead using a stand mixer on medium-low speed for 6-8 minutes.
5. **First Rise (Bulk Fermentation):**
    - Place the kneaded dough in a lightly oiled bowl, turning once to coat. Cover with plastic wrap or a kitchen towel and let it rise in a warm, draft-free place for about 1 to 1.5 hours, or until doubled in size.
6. **Shaping:**
    - After the dough has risen, punch it down gently to deflate. Shape it into a loaf and place it in a greased 9x5-inch loaf pan. Optionally, you can dust the pan with cornmeal for added texture.
7. **Second Rise:**
    - Cover the loaf pan loosely with plastic wrap or a kitchen towel and let it rise again for about 30-45 minutes, or until puffed up and nearly doubled in size.
8. **Preheat Oven:**
    - About 20 minutes before baking, preheat your oven to 375°F (190°C).

9. **Bake:**
    - Bake the Anadama bread in the preheated oven for 30-35 minutes, or until it is golden brown on top and sounds hollow when tapped on the bottom.
10. **Cool and Serve:**
    - Remove the baked Anadama bread from the loaf pan and transfer it to a wire rack to cool completely before slicing.

Tips:

- **Variations:** Some recipes include adding raisins or nuts to the dough for added flavor and texture.
- **Storage:** Store leftover Anadama bread in an airtight container or wrapped tightly in foil at room temperature for up to 3 days. It can also be frozen; slice it before freezing for easier reheating.

Enjoy your homemade Anadama bread sliced and toasted with butter, or as a complement to soups and stews. Its unique flavor from the molasses and cornmeal makes it a comforting choice for any occasion!

Cinnamon Swirl Bread

Ingredients:

For the Bread Dough:

- 1 cup warm milk (about 110°F/45°C)
- 1/4 cup granulated sugar
- 2 and 1/4 teaspoons (1 packet) active dry yeast
- 1/4 cup unsalted butter, melted
- 1 teaspoon salt
- 2 large eggs
- 4 cups bread flour (plus extra for kneading)

For the Cinnamon Swirl:

- 1/2 cup packed light brown sugar
- 2 tablespoons ground cinnamon
- 2 tablespoons unsalted butter, softened

Instructions:

1. **Activate Yeast:**
   - In a small bowl, combine the warm milk and granulated sugar. Sprinkle the yeast over the mixture and let it sit for about 5-10 minutes until frothy.
2. **Mix Dough:**
   - In a large mixing bowl or the bowl of a stand mixer fitted with a dough hook, combine the melted butter, salt, eggs, and bread flour.
   - Add the activated yeast mixture to the flour mixture and mix until a dough forms.
3. **Kneading:**
   - Turn the dough out onto a lightly floured surface and knead for about 8-10 minutes, or until the dough is smooth and elastic. Alternatively, knead using a stand mixer on medium-low speed for 6-8 minutes.
4. **First Rise (Bulk Fermentation):**
   - Place the kneaded dough in a lightly oiled bowl, turning once to coat. Cover with plastic wrap or a kitchen towel and let it rise in a warm, draft-free place for about 1 to 1.5 hours, or until doubled in size.
5. **Prepare Cinnamon Swirl:**
   - In a small bowl, mix together the brown sugar and ground cinnamon for the swirl.
6. **Shaping:**
   - After the dough has risen, punch it down gently to deflate. Roll out the dough on a lightly floured surface into a rectangle about 9x18 inches.
7. **Assembly:**
   - Spread the softened butter evenly over the rolled-out dough.

- Sprinkle the cinnamon sugar mixture evenly over the buttered dough, leaving a small border around the edges.
8. **Rolling:**
    - Starting from one of the long edges, tightly roll up the dough into a log. Pinch the seam to seal.
9. **Second Rise:**
    - Place the rolled log seam side down in a greased 9x5-inch loaf pan. Cover loosely with plastic wrap or a kitchen towel and let it rise again for about 30-45 minutes, or until puffed up and nearly doubled in size.
10. **Preheat Oven:**
    - About 20 minutes before baking, preheat your oven to 350°F (175°C).
11. **Bake:**
    - Bake the cinnamon swirl bread in the preheated oven for 30-35 minutes, or until it is golden brown on top and sounds hollow when tapped on the bottom.
12. **Cool and Serve:**
    - Remove the baked bread from the loaf pan and transfer it to a wire rack to cool completely before slicing.

Tips:

- **Variations:** You can add chopped nuts or raisins to the cinnamon sugar mixture for additional flavor and texture.
- **Storage:** Store leftover cinnamon swirl bread in an airtight container or wrapped tightly in foil at room temperature for up to 3 days. It can also be frozen; slice it before freezing for easier reheating.

Enjoy your homemade cinnamon swirl bread warm or toasted, perhaps with a smear of butter or cream cheese. Its comforting cinnamon aroma and sweet swirls make it a favorite for breakfast or anytime you crave something cozy!

Hokkaido Milk Bread

Ingredients:

Tangzhong (Starter):

- 1/3 cup bread flour
- 1 cup water

Main Dough:

- 2 and 1/2 cups bread flour
- 1/4 cup granulated sugar
- 1 teaspoon salt
- 2 teaspoons active dry yeast
- 1/2 cup warm milk (about 110°F/45°C)
- 1 large egg
- 1/4 cup unsalted butter, softened

Instructions:

Step 1: Make Tangzhong (Starter)

1. In a small saucepan, whisk together the bread flour and water until smooth.
2. Cook over medium heat, stirring constantly with a wooden spoon or whisk, until the mixture thickens to a pudding-like consistency (about 3-5 minutes).
3. Remove from heat and transfer to a clean bowl. Cover with plastic wrap, pressing the wrap directly onto the surface of the tangzhong to prevent a skin from forming. Let it cool to room temperature.

Step 2: Prepare Dough

1. In a large mixing bowl or the bowl of a stand mixer fitted with a dough hook, combine the bread flour, sugar, salt, and yeast.
2. Add the warm milk, egg, and tangzhong to the flour mixture. Mix on low speed until a rough dough forms.
3. Increase the speed to medium-low and knead the dough for about 5 minutes, until it becomes smooth and elastic.
4. Add the softened butter, a tablespoon at a time, kneading well after each addition until fully incorporated. Continue kneading for another 10-15 minutes until the dough is very smooth, shiny, and elastic. It should pass the windowpane test.

Step 3: First Rise

1. Shape the dough into a ball and place it in a lightly greased bowl, turning once to coat.

2. Cover the bowl with plastic wrap or a kitchen towel and let it rise in a warm, draft-free place for 1 to 1.5 hours, or until doubled in size.

Step 4: Shape and Second Rise

1. After the first rise, gently deflate the dough by pressing it down.
2. Divide the dough into equal portions (about 4-6 pieces, depending on the size of loaves you want).
3. Shape each portion into a ball or oval and place them in a greased loaf pan or on a baking sheet lined with parchment paper, leaving some space between them.
4. Cover loosely with plastic wrap or a kitchen towel and let them rise again for 45 minutes to 1 hour, until puffed up and nearly doubled in size.

Step 5: Baking

1. Preheat your oven to 350°F (175°C) during the last 15 minutes of the second rise.
2. Optional: Brush the tops of the loaves with a little milk or egg wash (1 egg beaten with 1 tablespoon of water) for a shiny crust.
3. Bake the loaves in the preheated oven for 25-30 minutes, or until they are golden brown on top and sound hollow when tapped on the bottom.
4. If using a thermometer, the internal temperature should reach about 190°F (88°C).

Step 6: Cooling and Serving

1. Remove the bread from the oven and let it cool in the pan for 5 minutes.
2. Transfer the loaves to a wire rack to cool completely before slicing.

Tips:

- **Variations:** You can add flavors like vanilla extract or incorporate fillings such as chocolate chips or nuts into the dough for added texture and flavor.
- **Storage:** Store leftover Hokkaido milk bread in an airtight container at room temperature for up to 3 days. It can also be frozen; slice it before freezing for easier reheating.

Enjoy your homemade Hokkaido milk bread sliced and toasted, or use it to make sandwiches and French toast. Its pillowy soft texture and subtle sweetness make it a favorite among bread enthusiasts!

Beer Bread

Ingredients:

- 3 cups all-purpose flour
- 1/4 cup granulated sugar (adjust to taste)
- 1 tablespoon baking powder
- 1 teaspoon salt
- 12 oz beer, at room temperature
- 1/4 cup unsalted butter, melted (for brushing on top, optional)

Instructions:

1. **Preheat Oven:**
   - Preheat your oven to 375°F (190°C). Grease a 9x5-inch loaf pan or line it with parchment paper.
2. **Mix Dry Ingredients:**
   - In a large bowl, whisk together the flour, sugar, baking powder, and salt until well combined.
3. **Add Beer:**
   - Pour the beer into the dry ingredients. Stir gently with a wooden spoon or spatula until just combined. The batter will be thick and sticky.
4. **Transfer to Loaf Pan:**
   - Scrape the batter into the prepared loaf pan and spread it evenly.
5. **Optional: Brush with Butter:**
   - If desired, brush the melted butter over the top of the batter before baking. This adds flavor and helps the crust brown nicely.
6. **Bake:**
   - Bake in the preheated oven for 45-55 minutes, or until the top is golden brown and a toothpick inserted into the center comes out clean.
7. **Cool and Serve:**
   - Remove the bread from the pan and transfer it to a wire rack to cool slightly before slicing and serving.

Tips:

- **Beer Selection:** Use a beer with a flavor profile you enjoy, as it will influence the taste of the bread. Pale ales, lagers, or even stout can work well.
- **Customization:** Feel free to add herbs, cheese, or even chopped nuts to the batter for added flavor and texture.
- **Storage:** Store leftover beer bread in an airtight container at room temperature for up to 3 days. It can also be frozen; wrap tightly in foil or plastic wrap before freezing.

Beer bread is perfect for serving alongside soups, stews, or simply enjoyed with butter as a snack. Its simplicity and delicious flavor make it a popular choice for quick homemade bread.

Jalapeño Cheddar Bread

Ingredients:

- 3 cups bread flour (plus extra for kneading)
- 1 tablespoon granulated sugar
- 1 tablespoon salt
- 1 tablespoon active dry yeast
- 1 cup warm water (about 110°F/45°C)
- 2 tablespoons olive oil
- 1 cup shredded cheddar cheese (plus extra for topping)
- 2-3 jalapeño peppers, seeded and finely chopped
- Optional: 1-2 tablespoons chopped fresh cilantro or parsley (for garnish)

Instructions:

1. **Activate Yeast:**
   - In a small bowl, combine the warm water and sugar. Sprinkle the yeast over the mixture and let it sit for about 5-10 minutes until frothy.
2. **Mix Dough:**
   - In a large mixing bowl or the bowl of a stand mixer fitted with a dough hook, combine the bread flour and salt.
   - Add the activated yeast mixture and olive oil to the flour mixture. Mix until a dough starts to form.
3. **Kneading:**
   - Turn the dough out onto a lightly floured surface and knead for about 8-10 minutes, or until the dough is smooth and elastic. Alternatively, knead using a stand mixer on medium-low speed for 6-8 minutes.
4. **Incorporate Cheese and Jalapeños:**
   - Flatten the kneaded dough and sprinkle the shredded cheddar cheese and chopped jalapeños evenly over the surface.
   - Fold the dough over itself and knead gently to distribute the cheese and jalapeños throughout the dough.
5. **First Rise (Bulk Fermentation):**
   - Place the kneaded dough in a lightly oiled bowl, turning once to coat. Cover with plastic wrap or a kitchen towel and let it rise in a warm, draft-free place for about 1 to 1.5 hours, or until doubled in size.
6. **Shaping:**
   - After the dough has risen, punch it down gently to deflate. Shape it into a round or oval loaf and place it on a parchment-lined baking sheet.
7. **Second Rise:**
   - Cover the shaped loaf loosely with plastic wrap or a kitchen towel and let it rise again for about 30-45 minutes, or until puffed up and nearly doubled in size.
8. **Preheat Oven:**

- About 20 minutes before baking, preheat your oven to 375°F (190°C).
9. **Optional Topping:**
   - If desired, sprinkle some extra shredded cheddar cheese and chopped cilantro or parsley on top of the risen loaf before baking.
10. **Bake:**
    - Bake the jalapeño cheddar bread in the preheated oven for 30-35 minutes, or until it is golden brown on top and sounds hollow when tapped on the bottom.
11. **Cool and Serve:**
    - Transfer the baked bread to a wire rack to cool completely before slicing.

Tips:

- **Handling Jalapeños:** Wear gloves when handling jalapeños, especially if you are sensitive to heat. Remove the seeds and membranes for milder heat, or leave them in for more spice.
- **Storage:** Store leftover jalapeño cheddar bread in an airtight container at room temperature for up to 3 days. It can also be frozen; slice it before freezing for easier reheating.

Enjoy your homemade jalapeño cheddar bread as a savory side to soups and salads, or toasted with butter for a delicious snack. Its cheesy goodness and subtle heat from the jalapeños make it a flavorful treat!

Onion Rye Bread

Ingredients:

- 1 cup warm water (about 110°F/45°C)
- 1 tablespoon granulated sugar
- 2 and 1/4 teaspoons (1 packet) active dry yeast
- 1/2 cup warm milk (about 110°F/45°C)
- 2 tablespoons unsalted butter, melted
- 1/4 cup molasses
- 1 tablespoon caraway seeds
- 2 teaspoons salt
- 1 cup rye flour
- 2 to 2 and 1/2 cups bread flour (plus extra for kneading)
- 1 cup finely chopped onions (about 1 medium onion)
- Olive oil (for greasing)
- Optional: Cornmeal or sesame seeds (for topping)

Instructions:

1. **Activate Yeast:**
   - In a small bowl, combine the warm water, sugar, and yeast. Let it sit for about 5-10 minutes until frothy.
2. **Mix Dough:**
   - In a large mixing bowl or the bowl of a stand mixer fitted with a dough hook, combine the yeast mixture, warm milk, melted butter, molasses, caraway seeds, and salt.
3. **Add Flours:**
   - Gradually add the rye flour and 2 cups of bread flour to the mixture, mixing until a rough dough forms.
4. **Kneading:**
   - Turn the dough out onto a lightly floured surface and knead for about 8-10 minutes, adding more bread flour as needed, until the dough is smooth and elastic. Alternatively, knead using a stand mixer on medium-low speed for 6-8 minutes.
5. **Incorporate Onions:**
   - Flatten the kneaded dough and sprinkle the finely chopped onions evenly over the surface.
   - Fold the dough over itself and knead gently to distribute the onions throughout the dough.
6. **First Rise (Bulk Fermentation):**
   - Place the kneaded dough in a lightly oiled bowl, turning once to coat. Cover with plastic wrap or a kitchen towel and let it rise in a warm, draft-free place for about 1 to 1.5 hours, or until doubled in size.

7. **Shaping:**
   - After the dough has risen, punch it down gently to deflate. Shape it into a round or oval loaf and place it on a parchment-lined baking sheet dusted with cornmeal or sesame seeds (if using).
8. **Second Rise:**
   - Cover the shaped loaf loosely with plastic wrap or a kitchen towel and let it rise again for about 30-45 minutes, or until puffed up and nearly doubled in size.
9. **Preheat Oven:**
   - About 20 minutes before baking, preheat your oven to 375°F (190°C).
10. **Bake:**
    - Bake the onion rye bread in the preheated oven for 30-35 minutes, or until it is golden brown on top and sounds hollow when tapped on the bottom.
11. **Cool and Serve:**
    - Transfer the baked bread to a wire rack to cool completely before slicing.

Tips:

- **Variations:** You can add more caraway seeds for extra flavor, or sprinkle some additional chopped onions on top before baking for a more pronounced onion taste.
- **Storage:** Store leftover onion rye bread in an airtight container at room temperature for up to 3 days. It can also be frozen; slice it before freezing for easier reheating.

Enjoy your homemade onion rye bread as a delicious accompaniment to soups, sandwiches, or simply toasted with butter. Its hearty texture and savory onion flavor make it a wonderful choice for any occasion!

Whole Wheat Baguettes

Ingredients:

- 2 cups whole wheat flour
- 1 cup bread flour (plus extra for kneading)
- 1 and 1/2 teaspoons salt
- 1 teaspoon active dry yeast
- 1 and 1/4 cups lukewarm water
- 1 tablespoon honey or sugar (optional, for a slightly sweeter flavor)
- Olive oil (for greasing)

Instructions:

1. **Activate Yeast:**
   - In a small bowl, combine the lukewarm water, honey (or sugar), and yeast. Stir gently and let it sit for about 5-10 minutes until frothy.
2. **Mix Dough:**
   - In a large mixing bowl or the bowl of a stand mixer fitted with a dough hook, combine the whole wheat flour, bread flour, and salt.
3. **Add Yeast Mixture:**
   - Pour the activated yeast mixture into the flour mixture. Mix until a rough dough forms.
4. **Kneading:**
   - Turn the dough out onto a lightly floured surface and knead for about 10-12 minutes, or until the dough is smooth and elastic. Add more bread flour as needed to prevent sticking. Alternatively, knead using a stand mixer on medium-low speed for 8-10 minutes.
5. **First Rise (Bulk Fermentation):**
   - Place the kneaded dough in a lightly oiled bowl, turning once to coat. Cover with plastic wrap or a kitchen towel and let it rise in a warm, draft-free place for about 1 to 1.5 hours, or until doubled in size.
6. **Divide and Shape:**
   - After the dough has risen, gently deflate it by pressing down on it. Divide the dough into two equal portions for two baguettes.
   - Shape each portion into a baguette shape: Flatten each piece of dough into a rectangle. Fold the long sides towards the center, overlapping slightly, and press to seal. Fold in half lengthwise and seal the seam by pinching it gently. Roll gently to elongate into a baguette shape, tapering the ends.
7. **Second Rise:**
   - Place the shaped baguettes on a parchment-lined baking sheet, leaving space between them. Cover loosely with plastic wrap or a kitchen towel and let them rise again for about 30-45 minutes, or until puffed up and nearly doubled in size.
8. **Preheat Oven:**

- About 20 minutes before baking, preheat your oven to 450°F (230°C). Place an empty baking pan on the bottom rack of the oven.

9. **Score and Bake:**
   - Using a sharp knife or a razor blade, make 3-4 diagonal slashes across the top of each baguette.
   - Optional: Spray or brush the baguettes with water before scoring to create a crisp crust.
   - Place the baking sheet with the baguettes in the preheated oven. Pour 1 cup of hot water into the empty baking pan on the bottom rack to create steam. This helps to develop a crusty exterior.

10. **Bake:**
    - Bake the baguettes for 20-25 minutes, or until they are golden brown and sound hollow when tapped on the bottom.

11. **Cool and Serve:**
    - Transfer the baked baguettes to a wire rack to cool completely before slicing.

Tips:

- **Flour Variations:** You can adjust the ratio of whole wheat flour to bread flour based on your preference. More bread flour will result in a lighter texture, while more whole wheat flour will yield a denser loaf with a nuttier flavor.
- **Storage:** Store leftover whole wheat baguettes in an airtight container or wrapped tightly in foil at room temperature for up to 3 days. They can also be frozen; slice them before freezing for easier reheating.

Enjoy your homemade whole wheat baguettes warm from the oven, sliced and dipped in olive oil, or as a base for sandwiches and bruschetta. Their rustic appearance and hearty flavor make them a delightful addition to any meal!

Sourdough English Muffins

Ingredients:

- 1 cup active sourdough starter (100% hydration)
- 1 cup lukewarm milk (about 110°F/45°C)
- 3 cups bread flour (plus extra for dusting)
- 1 tablespoon granulated sugar
- 1 teaspoon salt
- Cornmeal (for dusting)

Instructions:

1. **Prepare Dough:**
   - In a large mixing bowl or the bowl of a stand mixer fitted with a dough hook, combine the active sourdough starter and lukewarm milk. Stir until well combined.
2. **Add Dry Ingredients:**
   - Add the bread flour, sugar, and salt to the bowl. Mix until a rough dough forms.
3. **Kneading:**
   - If using a stand mixer, knead the dough on low speed for about 5-7 minutes until it becomes smooth and elastic. If kneading by hand, turn the dough out onto a lightly floured surface and knead for 10-12 minutes.
4. **First Rise (Bulk Fermentation):**
   - Place the kneaded dough in a lightly oiled bowl, turning once to coat. Cover with plastic wrap or a kitchen towel and let it rise in a warm, draft-free place for about 1.5 to 2 hours, or until doubled in size. Alternatively, you can let it rise overnight in the refrigerator for enhanced flavor.
5. **Shape and Cut:**
   - Turn the risen dough out onto a lightly floured surface. Gently deflate the dough and roll it out to a thickness of about 1/2 inch (1.25 cm).
   - Using a round cutter (about 3-4 inches in diameter), cut out rounds of dough. You can reroll the scraps to cut out more rounds.
6. **Second Rise:**
   - Place the cut-out muffins on a baking sheet dusted with cornmeal. Dust the tops lightly with more cornmeal. Cover loosely with plastic wrap or a kitchen towel and let them rise for about 45-60 minutes, or until puffed and slightly increased in size.
7. **Cooking:**
   - Heat a skillet or griddle over medium-low heat. Place the muffins on the skillet (you may need to do this in batches) and cook for about 7-10 minutes on each side, or until golden brown and cooked through.
   - Optionally, you can cook them on a baking sheet in the oven at 350°F (175°C) for 10-15 minutes after browning them on the griddle.

8. **Cool and Serve:**
    - Transfer the cooked English muffins to a wire rack to cool completely before slicing with a fork to preserve the nooks and crannies.

Tips:

- **Flavor Variation:** For additional flavor, you can add herbs, cheese, or even chopped nuts to the dough after the first rise.
- **Storage:** Store leftover sourdough English muffins in an airtight container at room temperature for up to 3 days. They can also be frozen; slice them before freezing for easier reheating.

Enjoy your homemade sourdough English muffins toasted and topped with butter, jam, or your favorite breakfast spread. Their tangy flavor and chewy texture make them a perfect morning treat!

Gluten-Free Bread

Ingredients:

- 2 cups gluten-free all-purpose flour blend (ensure it includes xanthan gum or add 1 teaspoon if not included)
- 1 cup gluten-free oat flour (you can grind gluten-free oats in a blender to make flour)
- 1/2 cup almond flour
- 1/4 cup ground flaxseed meal
- 2 teaspoons active dry yeast
- 1 teaspoon salt
- 1 tablespoon honey or maple syrup (for sweetness and yeast activation)
- 1 and 1/2 cups warm water (about 110°F/45°C)
- 2 tablespoons olive oil or melted coconut oil
- 3 large eggs, at room temperature
- Optional: Seeds (like sunflower, pumpkin, or sesame) for topping

Instructions:

1. **Activate Yeast:**
   - In a small bowl, combine the warm water, honey (or maple syrup), and yeast. Stir gently and let it sit for about 5-10 minutes until frothy.
2. **Mix Dry Ingredients:**
   - In a large mixing bowl, whisk together the gluten-free all-purpose flour blend, oat flour, almond flour, ground flaxseed meal, and salt.
3. **Combine Wet Ingredients:**
   - In a separate bowl, whisk together the olive oil (or melted coconut oil) and eggs.
4. **Mix Dough:**
   - Add the activated yeast mixture and the wet ingredients to the dry ingredients. Mix until well combined. The dough will be sticky and thicker than traditional bread dough.
5. **First Rise (Proofing):**
   - Transfer the dough into a greased loaf pan (about 9x5 inches). Smooth the top with a spatula dipped in water or oil.
   - Cover loosely with plastic wrap or a kitchen towel and let it rise in a warm, draft-free place for about 30-45 minutes, or until it has risen slightly. The dough may not double in size like traditional wheat dough.
6. **Preheat Oven:**
   - About 20 minutes before baking, preheat your oven to 350°F (175°C).
7. **Optional Topping:**
   - If desired, sprinkle seeds (such as sunflower, pumpkin, or sesame seeds) over the top of the loaf.
8. **Bake:**

- Bake the gluten-free bread in the preheated oven for 40-50 minutes, or until it is golden brown on top and sounds hollow when tapped on the bottom.

9. **Cool and Serve:**
   - Remove the bread from the loaf pan and transfer it to a wire rack to cool completely before slicing. Gluten-free bread can be more fragile than traditional bread, so allow it to cool completely for best slicing results.

Tips:

- **Flour Variations:** Experiment with different gluten-free flour blends based on your preferences and dietary needs. Some blends may include ingredients like rice flour, tapioca starch, or potato starch.
- **Binding Agents:** If your gluten-free flour blend doesn't contain xanthan gum or guar gum, you may need to add 1-2 teaspoons to help bind the dough together.
- **Storage:** Store leftover gluten-free bread in an airtight container at room temperature for up to 3 days. It can also be frozen; slice it before freezing for easier reheating.

Enjoy your homemade gluten-free bread sliced and toasted, or use it for sandwiches and to accompany soups and salads. Adjust the recipe to suit your taste preferences and dietary requirements for a satisfying gluten-free baking experience!

Spelt Bread

Ingredients:

- 3 cups whole grain spelt flour
- 1 cup bread flour (or all-purpose flour)
- 1 and 1/2 teaspoons salt
- 1 tablespoon honey or maple syrup
- 2 teaspoons active dry yeast
- 1 and 1/4 cups warm water (about 110°F/45°C)
- 2 tablespoons olive oil or melted butter
- Optional: Seeds (such as sunflower, sesame, or poppy seeds) for topping

Instructions:

1. **Activate Yeast:**
   - In a small bowl, combine the warm water, honey (or maple syrup), and yeast. Stir gently and let it sit for about 5-10 minutes until frothy.
2. **Mix Dough:**
   - In a large mixing bowl or the bowl of a stand mixer fitted with a dough hook, combine the spelt flour, bread flour (or all-purpose flour), and salt.
   - Add the activated yeast mixture and olive oil (or melted butter) to the flour mixture. Mix until a rough dough forms.
3. **Kneading:**
   - Turn the dough out onto a lightly floured surface and knead for about 8-10 minutes, or until the dough is smooth and elastic. Alternatively, knead using a stand mixer on medium-low speed for 6-8 minutes.
4. **First Rise (Bulk Fermentation):**
   - Place the kneaded dough in a lightly oiled bowl, turning once to coat. Cover with plastic wrap or a kitchen towel and let it rise in a warm, draft-free place for about 1 to 1.5 hours, or until doubled in size.
5. **Shaping:**
   - After the dough has risen, gently deflate it by pressing down on it. Shape it into a loaf by rolling it into a rectangle and then rolling it tightly from one end to the other. Pinch the seams and tuck the ends under.
6. **Second Rise:**
   - Place the shaped loaf in a greased loaf pan (about 9x5 inches). Cover loosely with plastic wrap or a kitchen towel and let it rise again for about 30-45 minutes, or until puffed up and nearly doubled in size.
7. **Preheat Oven:**
   - About 20 minutes before baking, preheat your oven to 375°F (190°C).
8. **Optional Topping:**
   - If desired, brush the top of the loaf with water and sprinkle seeds (such as sunflower, sesame, or poppy seeds) on top.

9. **Bake:**
   - Bake the spelt bread in the preheated oven for 35-40 minutes, or until it is golden brown on top and sounds hollow when tapped on the bottom.
10. **Cool and Serve:**
    - Remove the baked bread from the loaf pan and transfer it to a wire rack to cool completely before slicing.

Tips:

- **Flour Substitution:** You can adjust the ratio of spelt flour to bread flour (or all-purpose flour) based on your preference for a lighter or denser loaf.
- **Storage:** Store leftover spelt bread in an airtight container at room temperature for up to 3 days. It can also be frozen; slice it before freezing for easier reheating.

Enjoy your homemade spelt bread toasted with butter, as a base for sandwiches, or alongside soups and salads. Its hearty flavor and nutritional benefits make it a wonderful choice for homemade bread enthusiasts!

Lavash Crackers

Ingredients:

- 2 cups all-purpose flour
- 1 teaspoon salt
- 1 teaspoon sugar
- 1 teaspoon instant yeast
- 3/4 cup warm water
- 2 tablespoons olive oil
- Optional toppings: sesame seeds, poppy seeds, flaky sea salt, dried herbs (like thyme or rosemary), or spices (like smoked paprika or cumin)

Instructions:

1. **Prepare the Dough:**
   - In a large mixing bowl, whisk together the flour, salt, sugar, and instant yeast.
   - Add the warm water and olive oil to the flour mixture. Stir until a rough dough forms.
2. **Knead the Dough:**
   - Turn the dough out onto a lightly floured surface and knead for about 5-7 minutes, or until the dough is smooth and elastic. Alternatively, knead using a stand mixer fitted with a dough hook on medium speed for 4-5 minutes.
3. **First Rise:**
   - Place the kneaded dough in a lightly oiled bowl, turning once to coat. Cover with plastic wrap or a kitchen towel and let it rest at room temperature for about 1 hour, or until it has doubled in size.
4. **Preheat Oven:**
   - Preheat your oven to 400°F (200°C). Line one or two baking sheets with parchment paper.
5. **Divide and Roll Out the Dough:**
   - Punch down the risen dough and divide it into 4 equal portions.
   - On a lightly floured surface, roll out one portion of the dough as thinly as possible, aiming for a rectangle or oval shape. The thinner you roll it, the crispier the crackers will be.
   - Transfer the rolled-out dough to the prepared baking sheet. Repeat with the remaining portions of dough, placing each rolled-out piece on a separate baking sheet or using one baking sheet at a time if space is limited.
6. **Add Toppings (Optional):**
   - Brush the rolled-out dough with water and sprinkle with sesame seeds, poppy seeds, flaky sea salt, dried herbs, or spices if desired. Press them gently into the dough to adhere.
7. **Bake the Lavash Crackers:**

- Bake in the preheated oven for 10-12 minutes, or until the crackers are golden brown and crispy. Keep an eye on them towards the end of baking, as they can quickly go from golden to burnt.

8. **Cool and Break into Pieces:**
    - Remove the baked lavash crackers from the oven and let them cool completely on a wire rack. Once cooled, break them into irregular pieces or cut them into squares or rectangles using a sharp knife.

9. **Serve or Store:**
    - Serve the lavash crackers immediately or store them in an airtight container at room temperature for up to 1 week. They can also be frozen for longer storage; thaw at room temperature before serving.

Tips:

- **Customization:** Experiment with different toppings and seasonings to customize your lavash crackers. You can also sprinkle them with grated Parmesan cheese or za'atar for added flavor.
- **Storage:** To maintain crispiness, store lavash crackers in a single layer or with parchment paper between layers to prevent them from sticking together.

Enjoy your homemade lavash crackers with hummus, cheese, dips, or simply as a crunchy snack. They are versatile and perfect for entertaining or enjoying with a variety of toppings!

Swedish Cardamom Bread

Dough Ingredients:

- 1 cup milk
- 1/4 cup unsalted butter
- 1/4 cup granulated sugar
- 2 teaspoons active dry yeast
- 1/2 teaspoon salt
- 1 teaspoon ground cardamom (or seeds from about 15-20 cardamom pods, crushed and finely ground)
- 3 cups all-purpose flour (plus extra for kneading)

Filling Ingredients:

- 1/4 cup unsalted butter, softened
- 1/4 cup granulated sugar
- 1 tablespoon ground cardamom

Optional Topping:

- Pearl sugar or sliced almonds (for sprinkling on top before baking)

Instructions:

1. **Warm the Milk and Butter:**
   - In a small saucepan, heat the milk and butter over medium heat until the butter is melted. Remove from heat and let it cool until it reaches about 110°F (45°C), warm but not hot.
2. **Activate Yeast:**
   - In a large mixing bowl, combine the warm milk-butter mixture with the sugar and yeast. Stir gently and let it sit for about 5-10 minutes until the yeast is foamy.
3. **Mix Dough:**
   - Add the salt, ground cardamom, and 3 cups of flour to the yeast mixture. Stir until a rough dough forms.
4. **Knead the Dough:**
   - Turn the dough out onto a lightly floured surface and knead for about 8-10 minutes, or until the dough is smooth and elastic. Add more flour as needed if the dough is too sticky.
   - Alternatively, knead using a stand mixer fitted with a dough hook on medium speed for 6-8 minutes.
5. **First Rise (Bulk Fermentation):**

- Place the kneaded dough in a lightly oiled bowl, turning once to coat. Cover with plastic wrap or a kitchen towel and let it rise in a warm, draft-free place for about 1 to 1.5 hours, or until doubled in size.

6. **Prepare Filling:**
   - In a small bowl, mix together the softened butter, granulated sugar, and ground cardamom until well combined.
7. **Shape the Buns:**
   - Punch down the risen dough to deflate it. Roll the dough out into a rectangle about 12x16 inches.
   - Spread the cardamom filling evenly over the dough rectangle, leaving a small border around the edges.
   - Starting from one of the longer sides, roll the dough tightly into a log. Pinch the seam to seal.
   - Cut the log into 12 equal pieces (about 1 inch wide each). Place the pieces cut-side up in a greased or lined baking pan (or two pans if needed), leaving space between each piece for rising.
8. **Second Rise:**
   - Cover the baking pan(s) loosely with plastic wrap or a kitchen towel and let the buns rise again for about 30-45 minutes, or until puffed up and nearly doubled in size.
9. **Preheat Oven:**
   - About 20 minutes before baking, preheat your oven to 375°F (190°C).
10. **Optional Topping:**
    - If desired, sprinkle pearl sugar or sliced almonds over the tops of the buns before baking.
11. **Bake:**
    - Bake the Swedish Cardamom Buns in the preheated oven for 18-22 minutes, or until they are golden brown on top and sound hollow when tapped on the bottom.
12. **Cool and Serve:**
    - Remove the buns from the oven and let them cool slightly in the pan before transferring to a wire rack to cool completely.

Tips:

- **Variations:** You can add raisins or chopped nuts to the filling for added texture and flavor.
- **Storage:** Store leftover Swedish Cardamom Buns in an airtight container at room temperature for up to 3 days. They can also be frozen; thaw at room temperature before serving or reheating in the oven briefly.

Enjoy your homemade Swedish Cardamom Bread warm or at room temperature with a cup of coffee or tea. The delightful aroma of cardamom and the buttery sweetness of the filling make these buns a favorite treat for any occasion!

Lemon Poppy Seed Bread

Ingredients:

- 1 and 1/2 cups all-purpose flour
- 1 teaspoon baking powder
- 1/4 teaspoon baking soda
- 1/2 teaspoon salt
- Zest of 2 lemons
- 1 tablespoon poppy seeds
- 1/2 cup unsalted butter, softened
- 1 cup granulated sugar
- 2 large eggs, at room temperature
- 1 teaspoon vanilla extract
- 1/2 cup plain Greek yogurt or sour cream
- 1/4 cup fresh lemon juice (about 2 lemons)

Lemon Glaze (Optional):

- 1/2 cup powdered sugar
- 1-2 tablespoons fresh lemon juice

Instructions:

1. **Preheat Oven:**
   - Preheat your oven to 350°F (175°C). Grease and flour a 9x5-inch loaf pan or line it with parchment paper for easy removal.
2. **Dry Ingredients:**
   - In a medium bowl, whisk together the flour, baking powder, baking soda, salt, lemon zest, and poppy seeds. Set aside.
3. **Cream Butter and Sugar:**
   - In a large mixing bowl or the bowl of a stand mixer fitted with the paddle attachment, cream together the softened butter and granulated sugar until light and fluffy, about 2-3 minutes.
4. **Add Eggs and Vanilla:**
   - Add the eggs one at a time, mixing well after each addition. Stir in the vanilla extract.
5. **Combine Wet and Dry Ingredients:**
   - Gradually add the flour mixture to the butter mixture, alternating with the Greek yogurt (or sour cream), beginning and ending with the flour mixture. Mix until just combined.
6. **Add Lemon Juice:**
   - Fold in the fresh lemon juice until evenly incorporated into the batter. Be careful not to overmix.

7. **Bake:**
   - Pour the batter into the prepared loaf pan and spread it evenly with a spatula.
   - Bake in the preheated oven for 45-55 minutes, or until a toothpick inserted into the center of the bread comes out clean or with a few moist crumbs.
8. **Cool:**
   - Allow the lemon poppy seed bread to cool in the pan for about 15 minutes, then remove it from the pan and transfer it to a wire rack to cool completely.
9. **Optional Lemon Glaze:**
   - If desired, prepare the lemon glaze by whisking together powdered sugar and fresh lemon juice until smooth. Drizzle the glaze over the cooled bread.
10. **Slice and Serve:**
    - Once the glaze has set (if using), slice the lemon poppy seed bread and serve. Enjoy it with a cup of tea or coffee!

Tips:

- **Zesting Lemons:** Use a fine grater or zester to remove only the outer yellow peel of the lemons. Avoid grating the bitter white pith beneath the peel.
- **Storage:** Store leftover lemon poppy seed bread in an airtight container at room temperature for up to 3 days. It can also be frozen; wrap slices tightly in plastic wrap and store in a freezer-safe bag for up to 3 months.

Enjoy the bright and refreshing flavor of homemade lemon poppy seed bread, perfect for breakfast, brunch, or as a delightful snack any time of day!

Pistachio Cranberry Bread

Ingredients:

- 1 and 1/2 cups all-purpose flour
- 1 teaspoon baking powder
- 1/4 teaspoon baking soda
- 1/2 teaspoon salt
- 1/2 cup unsalted pistachios, chopped
- 1/2 cup dried cranberries
- 1/2 cup unsalted butter, softened
- 3/4 cup granulated sugar
- 2 large eggs, at room temperature
- 1 teaspoon vanilla extract
- 1/2 cup plain Greek yogurt or sour cream
- 1/4 cup milk

Optional Glaze:

- 1/2 cup powdered sugar
- 1-2 tablespoons milk or fresh lemon juice

Instructions:

1. **Preheat Oven:**
   - Preheat your oven to 350°F (175°C). Grease and flour a 9x5-inch loaf pan or line it with parchment paper for easy removal.
2. **Dry Ingredients:**
   - In a medium bowl, whisk together the flour, baking powder, baking soda, and salt.
3. **Add Pistachios and Cranberries:**
   - Toss the chopped pistachios and dried cranberries with 1 tablespoon of the flour mixture. This prevents them from sinking to the bottom of the bread while baking. Set aside.
4. **Cream Butter and Sugar:**
   - In a large mixing bowl or the bowl of a stand mixer fitted with the paddle attachment, cream together the softened butter and granulated sugar until light and fluffy, about 2-3 minutes.
5. **Add Eggs and Vanilla:**
   - Add the eggs one at a time, mixing well after each addition. Stir in the vanilla extract.
6. **Combine Wet and Dry Ingredients:**
   - Gradually add the flour mixture to the butter mixture, alternating with the Greek yogurt (or sour cream) and milk, beginning and ending with the flour mixture. Mix until just combined.

7. **Fold in Pistachios and Cranberries:**
    - Gently fold in the flour-coated pistachios and cranberries until evenly distributed in the batter.
8. **Bake:**
    - Pour the batter into the prepared loaf pan and spread it evenly with a spatula.
    - Bake in the preheated oven for 50-60 minutes, or until a toothpick inserted into the center of the bread comes out clean or with a few moist crumbs.
9. **Cool:**
    - Allow the pistachio cranberry bread to cool in the pan for about 15 minutes, then remove it from the pan and transfer it to a wire rack to cool completely.
10. **Optional Glaze:**
    - If desired, prepare the glaze by whisking together powdered sugar and milk (or fresh lemon juice) until smooth. Drizzle the glaze over the cooled bread.
11. **Slice and Serve:**
    - Once the glaze has set (if using), slice the pistachio cranberry bread and serve. Enjoy it with a cup of tea or coffee!

Tips:

- **Nuts and Fruit:** Feel free to adjust the amount of pistachios and cranberries to suit your taste preferences.
- **Storage:** Store leftover pistachio cranberry bread in an airtight container at room temperature for up to 3 days. It can also be frozen; wrap slices tightly in plastic wrap and store in a freezer-safe bag for up to 3 months.

Enjoy the delightful combination of flavors and textures in homemade pistachio cranberry bread, perfect for breakfast, brunch, or as a tasty snack!

Chocolate Babka

Dough Ingredients:

- 3 and 1/2 cups all-purpose flour
- 1/2 cup granulated sugar
- 1 tablespoon instant yeast
- 1 teaspoon salt
- 3 large eggs, at room temperature
- 1/2 cup warm milk
- 1/2 cup unsalted butter, softened
- 1 teaspoon vanilla extract

Chocolate Filling Ingredients:

- 1 cup semi-sweet chocolate chips or chopped chocolate
- 1/2 cup unsalted butter
- 1/2 cup powdered sugar
- 1/2 cup unsweetened cocoa powder

Optional Syrup Glaze:

- 1/2 cup water
- 1/2 cup granulated sugar

Instructions:

1. **Make the Dough:**
   - In a large mixing bowl or the bowl of a stand mixer fitted with the dough hook, combine 3 cups of flour, sugar, instant yeast, and salt.
   - In a separate bowl, whisk together the eggs, warm milk, softened butter, and vanilla extract.
   - Gradually add the wet ingredients to the dry ingredients and mix until a soft dough forms, adding more flour as needed if the dough is too sticky.
   - Knead the dough for about 8-10 minutes by hand on a lightly floured surface or with a stand mixer on medium-low speed until smooth and elastic.
   - Place the dough in a lightly oiled bowl, cover with plastic wrap or a kitchen towel, and let it rise in a warm, draft-free place for about 1 to 1.5 hours, or until doubled in size.
2. **Make the Chocolate Filling:**
   - In a heatproof bowl, melt together the chocolate chips (or chopped chocolate) and butter in the microwave or over a double boiler until smooth.
   - Stir in the powdered sugar and cocoa powder until well combined and smooth. Set aside to cool slightly.

3. **Assembly:**
   - Punch down the risen dough and roll it out on a lightly floured surface into a large rectangle, about 16x12 inches.
   - Spread the chocolate filling evenly over the dough rectangle, leaving a small border around the edges.
   - Starting from one of the longer sides, tightly roll up the dough into a log. Pinch the seam to seal.
   - Use a sharp knife to cut the log in half lengthwise, exposing the layers of filling.
   - Twist the two halves together, keeping the cut sides facing up to create a braided effect.
   - Carefully transfer the twisted dough into a greased 9x5-inch loaf pan, tucking the ends underneath.
4. **Second Rise:**
   - Cover the pan loosely with plastic wrap or a kitchen towel and let it rise again for about 30-45 minutes, or until puffed up and nearly doubled in size.
5. **Preheat Oven:**
   - About 20 minutes before baking, preheat your oven to 350°F (175°C).
6. **Bake:**
   - Bake the Chocolate Babka in the preheated oven for 30-35 minutes, or until it is golden brown on top and sounds hollow when tapped on the bottom.
7. **Optional Syrup Glaze:**
   - While the babka is baking, prepare the syrup glaze. In a small saucepan, combine water and sugar over medium heat. Bring to a boil, stirring until the sugar is dissolved. Remove from heat and set aside.
8. **Finish and Serve:**
   - Remove the babka from the oven and immediately brush the warm syrup glaze over the top of the bread.
   - Allow the babka to cool in the pan for about 15-20 minutes, then transfer it to a wire rack to cool completely before slicing and serving.

Tips:

- **Variations:** You can add chopped nuts (such as walnuts or pecans) to the filling for added texture and flavor.
- **Storage:** Store leftover Chocolate Babka in an airtight container at room temperature for up to 3 days. It can also be frozen; wrap slices tightly in plastic wrap and store in a freezer-safe bag for up to 3 months.

Enjoy the rich and indulgent flavors of homemade Chocolate Babka, perfect for breakfast, dessert, or as a special treat any time of day!

Stollen

Ingredients:

- 3/4 cup mixed dried fruits (such as raisins, currants, candied citrus peel)
- 1/4 cup rum or orange juice (for soaking dried fruits)
- 1/2 cup milk, lukewarm
- 2 and 1/4 teaspoons (1 packet) active dry yeast
- 1/4 cup granulated sugar
- 3 and 1/2 cups all-purpose flour
- 1/2 teaspoon salt
- 1/2 teaspoon ground cinnamon
- 1/4 teaspoon ground nutmeg
- 1/2 cup unsalted butter, softened
- 1 large egg
- 1/2 cup slivered almonds, toasted
- 1/2 cup candied or chopped almonds
- 1/2 cup raisins or sultanas
- 1/2 cup dried apricots, chopped
- 1/2 cup dried cranberries or cherries
- Zest of 1 lemon and 1 orange
- 1/2 cup marzipan (optional)
- Powdered sugar, for dusting

Instructions:

1. **Prepare the Dried Fruits:**
    - Place the mixed dried fruits in a small bowl and pour the rum or orange juice over them. Let them soak for at least 1 hour, or overnight, until plump and softened. Drain any excess liquid before using.
2. **Activate the Yeast:**
    - In a small bowl, combine the lukewarm milk, yeast, and a pinch of sugar. Stir gently and let it sit for about 5-10 minutes until the mixture is foamy.
3. **Make the Dough:**
    - In a large mixing bowl or the bowl of a stand mixer fitted with the dough hook, combine the flour, salt, cinnamon, nutmeg, and granulated sugar.
    - Add the softened butter, yeast mixture, and egg to the dry ingredients. Mix on low speed until the dough comes together.
    - Increase the speed to medium and knead the dough for about 8-10 minutes, or until it is smooth and elastic. If kneading by hand, this will take about 12-15 minutes.
4. **Incorporate Fruits and Nuts:**

- Add the soaked dried fruits, toasted slivered almonds, candied almonds, raisins or sultanas, chopped apricots, dried cranberries or cherries, lemon zest, and orange zest to the dough. Knead (or mix on low speed) until evenly distributed.

5. **Optional: Add Marzipan:**
   - If using marzipan, roll it into a log shape about 8 inches long. Flatten the Stollen dough into a rectangle and place the marzipan log in the center. Fold the dough over the marzipan and pinch the edges to seal.

6. **First Rise (Bulk Fermentation):**
   - Shape the dough into a ball and place it in a lightly oiled bowl, turning once to coat. Cover with plastic wrap or a kitchen towel and let it rise in a warm, draft-free place for about 1 to 1.5 hours, or until doubled in size.

7. **Shape and Second Rise:**
   - Punch down the risen dough to deflate it. Shape it into an oval or rectangular loaf, about 10-12 inches long.
   - Place the shaped Stollen on a parchment-lined baking sheet. Cover loosely with plastic wrap or a kitchen towel and let it rise again for about 30-45 minutes, or until puffed up and nearly doubled in size.

8. **Preheat Oven:**
   - About 20 minutes before baking, preheat your oven to 350°F (175°C).

9. **Bake:**
   - Bake the Stollen in the preheated oven for 35-45 minutes, or until it is golden brown and sounds hollow when tapped on the bottom.

10. **Cool and Dust with Powdered Sugar:**
    - Remove the Stollen from the oven and let it cool on a wire rack. While it is still warm, generously dust it with powdered sugar.

11. **Serve:**
    - Stollen is traditionally sliced and served at room temperature. Store any leftover Stollen in an airtight container at room temperature for up to 1 week, or freeze for longer storage.

Tips:

- **Aging:** Stollen improves with age. You can wrap it tightly in foil and let it rest for a few days before serving to allow the flavors to meld.
- **Variations:** Feel free to adjust the types of dried fruits and nuts to suit your preference.

Enjoy the festive and flavorful Stollen with a cup of tea or coffee, or as part of your holiday celebrations!

www.ingramcontent.com/pod-product-compliance
Lightning Source LLC
LaVergne TN
LVHW061939070526
838199LV00060B/3885